THE ESSENTIAL SURVIVAL MANUAL

THIS IS A CARLTON BOOK

This edition published in 2018 by
Carlton Books
20 Mortimer Street
London W1T 3JW

Copyright © 2002, 2018 Carlton Books Limited

This book is sold subject to the condition that it shall not, by way of
trade or otherwise, be lent, resold, hired out or otherwise circulated
without the publisher's prior written consent in any form of cover or
binding other than that in which it is published and without a similar
condition, including this condition, being imposed upon the subsequent
purchaser. All rights reserved.

ISBN: 978-1-78739-155-0

10 9 8 7 6 5 4 3 2 1

Printed in China

The material in this book was previously published in
The Essential Survival Guide

Dedications
To Mum and Dad, for never questioning where I was or what I was doing.
To my wife Alexandra and my girls, Kelly, Emily and Caroline, for keeping my feet on the ground, but not too much.

Acknowledgements
To the British Army, for paying me to train and giving me the opportunity to experience what it's like to survive armed conflict and to teach others to survive. To Sergeant Major Eddie McGee, for the times we spent together and the experience I gained from him. To the Royal Geographical Society, for the hours I have spent in the map-room planning my expeditions. To Captain Jonathon Barrington-Brookes-Ford, for his support, loyalty and the training we endured together. To Keele University's Education Department, for employing me to teach and study the effects of survival on the students who attended the lectures and ground training. To the Academy of Experts, Gray's Inn, London, for their extensive training in mediation and negotiation. To Sergeant Major Mike Beaman, for his support, and to Sergeant Major Brian Harding (Chick), for the close protection and evasive driving training.

A Prepper's Guide

THE ESSENTIAL SURVIVAL MANUAL

Expert Advice for Extreme Situations

KENN GRIFFITHS

CARLTON BOOKS

CONTENTS

Introduction: Mindset To Win 6

Survival 8

Prepper's Guide 10

The Psychology of Self-Defence 14

Communication 16

Developing Awareness 20

Shelters and Shelter-Building 21

Cold Climates 30

Surviving Cold, Wet Conditions 31

Surviving in Hot Conditions 33

Surviving Water 34

Surviving Fire 43

Street Survival 46

Self-Defence 49

Basic Defence Stance 51

Acts of Terror 64

Surviving Terrorism 73

New and Cyber Threats to Survival 78

Navigation on Land	85
Search and Rescue	96
Attracting Attention	107
International Distress Signalling	108
The Body's Needs	110
Cooking Fires	117
Cooking Methods	128
Primitive Equipment	130
Hunting and Trapping	132
What to Eat	138
Edible/Medicinal Plants	142
Surviving a Hitchhike	144
Travelling by Car	146
Travelling by Air and Sea	149
Escape and Evasion	153
First Aid	155
The Final Word: Death	174
Appendix	176

Mindset To Win

Over the years, the terms 'survival', 'survivalism' and 'survivalist' have become associated with gun-toting, muscle-bound macho figures, misunderstood rogue soldiers and military special forces personnel trained to penetrate deep into enemy territory. The media hype surrounding these characters has been further enhanced by the writings of former and currently serving military survival instructors. Despite this, the truth is that it is very ordinary people who have won the vast majority of successful fights against the odds and survived. And why not? Every day of our lives is a fight for survival.

Some of us survive the crime-ridden streets of major cities, others the remote jungles of Papua New Guinea. Throughout our lives we develop the skills needed to cope with the changing environments we live in. Many of us expand this knowledge to enable us to cope with – and live and work in – a wide variety of climatic, geographical and man-made extremes. Difficulties mainly arise when we are forced to survive in environments for which we are not mentally, emotionally or physically prepared. And yet, given a group of individuals in the same dangerous, life-threatening situation, without adequate knowledge or training, some will live through while others die. Some political prisoners who have been subjected to extreme torture, violence, starvation and other appalling conditions have lived while others with relatively minor ailments have given up and died. It has to be the case that the latter group lost their will to survive.

Many incidents of outstanding personal courage have demonstrated man's will to survive against all the odds. One particular act that underpins this is the true account of a lone working farmer who, having had his arm severed in some agricultural machinery, had the will and presence of mind to realize that if he collapsed he would die. He carried his severed arm a considerable distance to effect a self-rescue, and thereby saved his own life.

Experiences such as this are proof that survivors are not made, and that training alone is not sufficient to win the fight – mental attitude is more important! I have seen the biggest and hardest crumble under the pressure of survival encounters while stereotypical weaklings win a firm grip of the situation, and their existence.

Survival

The word 'survive' means to live on – to fight when all hope has gone. Fortunately, few of us will ever be in this position. In most cases the fight lasts just long enough for help to arrive. The difficulty lies in having the courage and will to stay alive long enough for rescuers to arrive, or to effect a self-rescue. In both cases, the survival priorities are the same, and can be listed in order of importance as:

· PROTECTION · LOCATION · WATER · FOOD

Throughout this book, we will discuss these priorities in detail, along with many more aspects of survival and personal safety.

Having some knowledge of survival and safety will be a benefit to you and those around you if you are ever in a life-threatening situation. Add in some training and specific experience, and your chances of survival will be even higher. In a potential survival situation, your most important priority is to recognize the immediate dangers and how to manage them effectively, while noting the longer-term potential dangers that can arise from poor judgement at this most crucial stage.

After injury, physical conditions – wind, wet and cold – account for most deaths in survival situations. The survivor's first priority has to be to protect against the elements, both current and future. The human body can produce its own heat, but body heat is rapidly removed by wind. This cooling effect, wind chill, becomes faster when the body is wet. Protection from hypothermia (fatally low body temperature) is paramount.

The sun can also bake you to death. Although hyperthermia is not as rapid as hypothermia, it is just as dangerous. In hot climates, you need to keep physical activities to a minimum during the hottest part of the day and shelter from the sun, preferably in a well-ventilated position. The need for clean drinking water is obvious.

Your physical condition also affects your efficiency, but a positive psychological approach will keep you alive even though you may have severe injuries. A good knowledge of first aid is a great advantage.

SET YOUR MIND TO WIN

Ignorance of survival skills leads to a dangerous lack of confidence. This can bring you to a state of panic, one of the most dangerous and life-threatening human responses there is. Once a person panics, rational thought gives way to illogical and irresponsible action. Even a little knowledge goes a long way towards averting panic.

From the very beginning of any survival situation, you must take control of yourself. Have the confidence to fight. Your subconscious holds a wealth of mental resources to help you develop the will to survive. Without it, you will most likely die. You have probably never consciously accessed that resolve, however, and you can work against it by convincing yourself that you can't win!

Be sure that you set your mind to 'win' mode. You can survive. You can win. Other people do, and so can you!

The will to survive is your first weapon in the fight against wind, cold, wet and heat. The struggle is with yourself. You have to battle against your physical condition, your lack of knowledge, fear, panic and your initial lack of confidence.

Once you have found the will to survive, your main aids to survival are inner strength, knowledge, the equipment you have or can find or manufacture, and your psychological approach. This latter is greatly enhanced by a sense of humour.

Never give up!

Never let anything get the better of you.

Never think you can't – know that you can.

Prepper's Guide

As with most things in life, the better prepared you are, the better the outcome. Just reading about survival techniques will give you an edge but getting down and practicing the skills and techniques gives you a definite advantage. Add to this pre-disaster planning and preparation and you lift your chances of survival to a much higher plain.

There's a well-known saying, especially in military circles, commonly known as the 6P's: "Proper Preparation Prevents Poor Performance" (note there are only five here – the sixth is a profanity!). The need to practise the physical skills is obvious. However, to enhance the survival effort further, there is an equally important need to ensure you have kit and equipment stored and ready to use in the event of a catastrophic event that takes away the normal infrastructure you rely on, even for a short time. You may think this is a step too far, but it is not unknown for power and water supplies to be "off-grid" in the most developed countries. Terrorists understand this, and the reliance of water in everyday life, so it is not beyond the realms of possibility that an attack to contaminate water and food supplies is on the agenda.

When travelling, always carry a small survival kit containing, as a minimum, the following: waterproof matches, small candle, craft knife blade, snare, fishing kit, pencil, paper, compass, signal mirror, whistle, flashlight, small multi-tool, water purifying tablets, condoms and a supply of personal medication. For a more prolonged survival effort you need to put together a comprehensive, "crash out" store of kit, often referred to as a "Bug Out Bag".

Where you store your survival "Bug Out Bag" is a matter for you but I would suggest that there is a need to consider having a "stash" hidden or buried in a secure but easily accessible location. No matter where you decide to store the kit, it must be in a place and container that can stand the extremes of weather and disaster. It would be futile to have it stashed away in a plastic container that would melt if fire was an issue, or float away if there happened to be a flash flood. Likewise, there's no point in storing equipment in a shed where it can be exposed to extreme temperatures, pilfered, or strewn across the garden following a hurricane. It may well be in place for some considerable time and, as such, it must be in a suitable state

Prepper's Guide

for keeping the contents clean, dry, serviceable and secure. For me, the best option is to bury a suitable container in a location where I can get at it without delay and without needing to compromise my security. An airtight polyethylene container with a screw-top, excellent resistance to most chemicals and a long shelf life is a good option. These are in commercial use all over the world, easy to obtain and manufactured in a variety of sizes to suit everyone's needs.

One drawback is the probability of condensation. To combat this, use a desiccant: a hygroscopic substance that induces a state of dryness by absorbing water. You can buy it or collect the packets of crystals found in a multitude of consumer items sent through the post or delivered to your door.

The following list of essential survival equipment is the starting point. Specialist air, sea and vehicle kits for use in expeditions, military encounters and remote working areas will include specific emergency equipment to enhance the basics.

To make sure you are on point when packing, keep to the rules of survival priority: Protection, Location, Water and Food.

Survival kits must be kept in a container that can stand the extremes of weather and disaster.

Prepper's Guide

PROTECTION
- ▲ **Waterproof copy of this book**
- ▲ **Lightweight, waterproof/windproof shell clothing and headwear, including bandana**
- ▲ **Head lamp**
- ▲ **Survival "Bivi" bag**
- ▲ **Emergency sleeping bag**
- ▲ **Emergency shelter equipment: tent and/or shelter building tarpaulin with eyelets and elastic cords**
- ▲ **Rope: 9mm multipurpose manmade fibre rope and "Para" cord (note: rope deteriorates, so test the elasticity before using to climb or abseil)**
- ▲ **First aid and medical emergency pack: Be sure to maintain items in date – creams, tablets, wipes, etc. have a limited shelf life. If you need long-term medicines, you may not be able to get them post-disaster. Look at natural alternatives: e.g. for migraine prevention, eat two feverfew leaves. They taste bitter but will help the condition. Many modern drugs have a direct link to natural remedies; learn how to prepare them and keep your knowledge up to date**

Recognizing and understanding medicinal plants is a basic survival skill.

- ▲ Flashlight (batteries don't store well, especially if left in the device. An alternative is the wind-up model)
- ▲ Weapon, ammunition and cleaning kit. Guns need to be prepared for long-term storage by covering in grease and then wrapping. Before you pack a gun, make sure it actually works! When it comes to crossbows and bolts, avoid natural material construction. The law relating to weaponry and its use varies so check the local situation. Clearly, where law and order has collapsed, it's a wholly different matter!
- ▲ Money: Cash is king, especially when the ATMs have been "taken out", so store a bundle of the local currency. Gold is recognized the world over; it has the benefit of not deteriorating over time and can be used if there is a currency crash.

LOCATION

- ▲ Compass, along with local maps, writing paper and pencils
- ▲ Wind-up radio
- ▲ Signalling equipment: distress beacon, whistle, mirror, high-visibility tape and plastic sheet, flares
- ▲ Tools: hatchet, knife, sharpening stone, flexible and/or folding saw, multipurpose tool.

WATER

- ▲ Sterile containers. Remember, condoms are sterile and can hold a large quantity of water
- ▲ Purifying equipment: Purifying tablets have a shelf life of approximately five years. Solar still, filter straws.

FOOD

- ▲ Trapping equipment: snares, fishing lines of various strengths, fish hooks, gillnet
- ▲ Salt (not table salt) is ideal for food preservation
- ▲ Fire lighting equipment: burning lens, flint and steel, candles (one match lights a candle, one candle can light many fires). Put cotton balls soaked in flammable jelly sealed in a plastic bag.

The Psychology of Self-Defence

Physical violence and aggression are not someone else's problem. They can and do affect anyone. The perpetrators of these crimes are indiscriminate in their selection of targets. Young or old, male or female, all are the same to the criminal who uses violence to control others.

We all have a right to live free of oppression. Safety from violence and aggression is a fundamental requirement for a full and enjoyable life. Sadly, some take great pleasure in stripping others of such basic rights. Every day of our lives has the potential to confront us with violence and aggression. We usually deal with potential violence by defusing the situation, by using our communication skills to find the aggressor's social conscience. Everyone has one – it's just that some are very distorted, often by the person's own violent early life experiences.

Once we find the aggressor's switch, we can either make things worse or turn the aggression away from physical violence. All things being equal, we achieve this by self-confidence. If we show a lack of confidence, we give the aggressor a signal of our uncertainty and vulnerability. Once this happens, any remaining negotiation is one-sided – his side! If we can continue to show confidence, we can often avoid physical confrontation. Good communication skills often move the interaction from a physical confrontation to a verbal settlement.

When the talking stops, or when you are stopped from talking, you may then have to resort to violence. Unfortunately, man is the main hunter of man. There are times when you have to fight back.

FIGHT TO SURVIVE

In the daily fight for survival, you may be confronted by a violent person who is intent on damaging or killing you. Physical violence is not pleasant, but neither is it an automatic disaster. Much depends on your ability to quickly alter your thinking and deal with the situation. Generally, fear of an attack is worse than the attack itself.

Once you have made the decision to fight – or have had the decision forced upon you – you must be absolutely determined to win. That means being as ruthless as you can be. Forget the sporting mentality. Aim to stop the aggressor, and give no mercy at all. It sounds extreme, I know, but if someone might be trying to kill you, you must conquer your own feelings of compassion

The Psychology of Self-Defence

and your distaste for violence and killing. If you must fight, fight with all your inner strength.

Be absolutely resolute when you have to defend against an attack. You must treat it as an attempt to take a life – and that means that you have to fight to kill the aggressor. Once the action starts, refuse to accept defeat and work hard to achieve victory. Put no rules on your action. Revert to absolute brutality. You are dealing with a life-threatening situation, and there is no room for scruples. The second you hesitate, the aggressor will take the initiative, and you will probably die.

FIGHT FIRE WITH FIRE

The average law-abiding person fears the consequence of taking violent defensive action. Throughout our lives, we are taught to respect the law and other people. That's fine for dealing with a normal, decent individual. But anyone who uses extreme violence clearly falls outside this category, and cannot be shown any mercy.

If you are confronted with violence, you do have the right to defend yourself with reasonable force. It is eminently reasonable to stop someone from killing you by killing them first!

Meeting violence with violence does not comes easily to most people. Having to fight for your life is psychologically damaging, even if you come out physically unscathed. This damage often remains long after the body has healed. Post-traumatic stress is a well-known condition, and there is excellent counselling available if you need support after an attack. Some consolation can come from knowing you were pushed into a situation of your aggressor's making, and had no choice. If you can put your hand on your heart and know you acted in self-defence, doing what you had to do to save yourself and/or others from harm or death, then truly you have nothing to feel guilty about.

Communication

We communicate to exchange information, ideas and feelings in a number of ways. In a survival situation, you are face to face with your aggressor. From the very moment of the first glimpse, communication has already started without a word being spoken. Through the eyes, the figure and facial features of the person are transmitted to the brain; within a millisecond, the picture joins that section of the brain that holds the schema of all the people you have met, seen and have had described to you. Without you realizing it, your body is already reacting – your body language is communicating with the other person.

You may never have met this person before, but he could fit a particular negative stereotype that you already have. He may be dressed in a way that shows his religious or political beliefs, or he may remind you of a person who has posed a threat to you in the past. Likewise, he will have already begun analyzing you in the same way. Understanding the way in which non-verbal communication works and adapting this may be the edge you need in order to interact verbally with a possible attacker or terrorist without antagonizing them or making yourself a target.

Non-verbal communication accounts for between 55% and 90% of everyday conversation. How the aggressor reacts to you will be greatly influenced by your body language and your tone of voice. Understanding the signs and being able to read them quickly will help you to react in a positive way and hopefully turn an aggressive confrontation into a two-way conversation.

When faced with the prospect of violence, the human body reacts by preparing you for either fighting or running. It's very difficult to control this reaction, and equally difficult to get rational control long enough to make a proper appraisal and adopt the most appropriate response. Being able to communicate effectively in these situations helps you to take control and lessen the risk of violence.

BEING ASSERTIVE

Assertive communication is about getting your point across and allowing the other person to put their point of view to you, without either party feeling threatened. If you are aggressive, this tells your opponents that you allow yourself the right of expression whilst denying them that same right. This can only result in escalating aggression and, ultimately, violence. Remember; in a survival situation your first priority must be protection, and that means avoiding violence at all costs. The key is to communicate with your opponent to the point where you and they have a feeling of mutual respect, even if it is false.

During my mediation and negotiation training, I learned how this mutual respect between hostage and captor can grow into virtual collusion. This is the Stockholm Syndrome, where the hostage actually starts to help the captor! I've witnessed similar situations with long-term undercover operators and the criminals they have been observing. Such agents can become a danger to their colleagues and jeopardize entire operations.

Similarly, if you can develop your communication skills as effectively, you may well be able to turn your captors into friends. This can help you avoid becoming a long-term hostage, or a victim murdered to prove a point.

NON-VERBAL CUES

Obviously, there are thousands of non-verbal indicators that can give you an indication of your opponent's true feelings. Some of the most common to watch for and to avoid are below.

> **Tilting the head down indicates the person is unsure.**
>
> **You:** You must avoid showing your opponent that you are unsure. Always present yourself as being confident and in control.
> **Them:** This signal indicates you have touched a vulnerable spot. Use the same line of conversation carefully to keep your opponent on their back foot.

Communication

> **Hand clenched as a fist across the chest is a sure sign of hostility.**
>
> **You:** Displaying your hostility to the other side is almost always counter-productive.
> **Them:** Be very careful; this person is clearly hostile towards you. If at all possible, keep out of their way. If you have to interact, give them room to be a little hostile, and be assertive to stop them from overstepping the mark. In a hostage situation, plan how to eliminate this person first or you may become a target.

> **Finger-jabbing shows that the person is becoming aggressive. If the jabbing escalates, they are becoming more agitated.**
>
> **You:** This gesture can inflame situations and enrage opponents. Keep your fingers to yourself!
> **Them:** Your communication is inflaming the situation, not defusing it. Try a different tack to calm the situation.

ASSERTIVE COMMUNICATION

In many situations, assertive communication can help avert violence. Many people confuse assertiveness with aggression, but the two are absolutely different. Aggressive conversation assumes the aggressor has more rights than the person they are communicating with, but assertive communication is about putting your point across while respecting the other person's right to their opinion and viewpoint.

When people communicate assertively, the conversation is a true exchange and real dialogue can take place. This often defuses a aggressive situations. Everyone should have the right to:

- ▲ **State their needs and make requests**
- ▲ **Set personal priorities**
- ▲ **Receive respect and dignity**
- ▲ **Express feelings, opinions and beliefs**

- ▲ **Freely agree, disagree and say 'yes' and 'no'**
- ▲ **Be treated as equal**
- ▲ **Be able to change their minds without ridicule or seeming weak**
- ▲ **Be allowed to make mistakes and to rethink positions**
- ▲ **Express lack of understanding and receive clear explanation**
- ▲ **State beliefs without feeling that they need approval**
- ▲ **Make decisions for themselves**
- ▲ **Accept – or refuse – responsibility for solving other people's problems**

Assertive communication is an enabling device. It gives people the room to manoeuvre without feeling that they are being seen as weaker. When the balance of communication is equal, negative and unpredictable emotions such as anger and fear can be replaced by constructive and positive responses. When this point has been reached, you can negotiate properly, and move away from aggression and violence.

Developing Awareness

People often seem to know when something bad is going to happen before it does, or when a person is a threat, or about to commit a crime. I believe that humans have developed a sense of personal security and are constantly subconsciously monitoring their environment and the people they meet. Whether it is psychic awareness or an evolutionary self-defence tool, people do have a real sense of danger: an internal warning mechanism. Always trust and act on your own feelings and instincts.

You can help to develop your awareness by taking more notice of your surroundings. When travelling, take the time to research the geography, geology, natural faults and weather patterns. You will avoid dangerous surprise if an earthquake or sudden typhoon hits.

Wherever you stay, look for the best escape route in case of fire or disaster. If you are in a high-rise building where you must follow signed emergency exits, walk the escape route and make sure that you know how to open any doors and negotiate other hazards. Removing obstructions may well save your life. If there is no realistic route to safety, ask to be moved to the ground floor. Check that windows and doors open easily. Also, ensure you can secure yourself in your room if there is any possibility of a violent encounter. Always make sure you have an escape route and a safe place to hide.

Wherever you are, be aware of the possible dangers. Make every effort to organize yourself, your room and your vehicles to give you the upper hand in an emergency. You may be inadvertently leaving weapons around for a chance attacker. Are your knives left out in the kitchen overnight? Imagine you are a burglar and have been surprised by the house occupants. You are in the kitchen, and there is a knife block by the bread board...

Be aware. Stay alive.

Shelters and Shelter-Building

A shelter is an object, position or location that provides an area of protection from the elements or some other danger. As well as providing physical protection, well-made shelters should offer the occupants as comfortable and as safe an environment as possible. This is difficult to achieve, especially in a hurriedly-constructed, makeshift shelter.

Nevertheless, you should aim to build a temporary dwelling that you can sleep in. In a survival situation, you become tired amazingly quickly, and even the simplest task requires mammoth physical and mental effort. The more sleep you get, the better your chances. Unfortunately, sleeping in survival situations is not easy. Always sleep when you are tired, and forget about your normal sleep patterns. Catnapping helps you to cope in hostile situations and environments, as well as conserving your energy.

Over the years, I have found that in the early stages of a survival situation it is easiest to sleep well during daylight. This is no problem, as long as you have done enough to sustain yourself. Trying to sleep at night in wet and cold conditions, with unfamiliar, threatening noises, can quickly sap your will. You are better off staying awake and tending the fire. This will keep you relatively warm and occupied, and you'll probably doze quite a lot, which will help to conserve your energy.

DETERMINING YOUR SHELTER TYPE

If you need to construct an emergency shelter somewhere remote, you will probably have arrived at your location by transport. It can be worth utilizing any vehicle, or its remains, when building your shelter. Do not use vehicles as shelters, though. They are usually made of metal, and will lethally act as a refrigerator in cold weather and an oven when it is hot. It is better to construct a shelter using a mixture of vehicle panels and interior fittings with local shelter-building materials. If you do decide to use a vehicle, make sure that it is free from hazards such as leaking fuel or precarious positioning.

You also have to consider whether or not you want to be found. You may be in politically hostile territory, where being found by the locals is dangerous. In such cases, move away from any wreckage or broken-down vehicles, as these can easily be spotted. Obviously, if you do want to be found, staying nearby will help.

In general terms, the type of shelter you need is determined by:
- **The elements which threaten you**
- **Your geographical location**
- **Materials you arrived with, local vegetation and geological features**
- **The length of time for which you anticipate staying – this can vary immensely**
- **Whether you wish to be found**
- **The number of people in the party, and their level of ability, fitness (physical and psychological) and injuries.**

FIRST CONSIDERATIONS

Your first consideration when building a shelter should be picking a suitable site. This is relatively easy on a nice, sunny day with plenty of time before sunset, but in reality your first shelter may merely be a hurriedly-constructed windbreak using a hollow or vegetation.

If you are at high altitude, you should try hard to move lower down. You will be less exposed, reducing the risk of freezing. However, unless you are sure that you can complete the move and that it is safe, stay where you are while you properly plan a descent. In any event, avoid following streams and rivers. These tend to find the quickest route down a hill or mountain – usually straight off a concealed cliff!

SHELTERS AND THE LANDSCAPE

Study your surroundings and take a close look at the geology. In limestone areas and rocky shorelines, you may find caves. These can make quick shelters, but be aware that they are usually formed by regular water, either from tides or underground rivers, and have a tendency to flood. If you do decide on a cave, remember that people and water do not usually mix! Also, many caves are already home to animals and insects – especially bats and bears.

Other rock formations can offer the basis of a decent shelter. Sedimentary rocks such as sandstones are often weathered, and have fissures and hollows that offer good protection. These features are made by prevailing winds and weather, so choose one with the elements in mind. Rocks may break off from time to time, especially if

Shelters and Shelter-Building

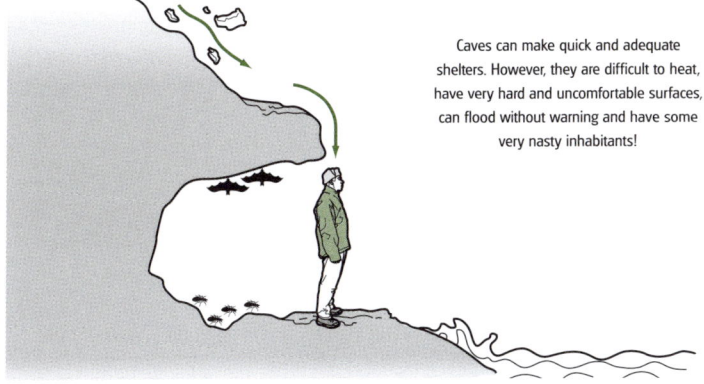

Caves can make quick and adequate shelters. However, they are difficult to heat, have very hard and uncomfortable surfaces, can flood without warning and have some very nasty inhabitants!

the days are hot and the nights freezing. If your site is in the shadow of high rocks, use natural, sturdy overhangs as a roof protection from falling fragments. If you cannot find adequate protection, build your shelter far enough away to avoid rock-falls.

Hard, igneous rocks, such as granite, usually contain horizontal cracks and joints formed during the rock's cooling, expanded by thousands of years of erosion. These can be the foundation of a good, safe shelter. However, such rocks are often highly magnetized, and may distort readings on your navigation instruments.

Using the rock's natural faults as a basis to build your shelter can be a very effective way of quickly establishing a position.

Shelters and Shelter-Building

WOODLAND SHELTERS

Woodland areas offer an ample supply of materials, but there are some issues you should note. Trees rot. They can become extremely unstable, and may shed bits as small as twigs or as large as huge boughs. In the worst case, the whole lot can come down without any prior warning. Rotten trees also harbour a great deal of insect life, which can be unpleasant – even dangerous.

Dead timber soon becomes weak, and is unsafe to use for shelter-building. It may seem fine when you construct the frame for your shelter, but will become very unstable with the weight of a shelter covering, especially when the covering is further weighed down with rainwater or a heavy fall of snow. Whenever possible, use only fresh, green, flexible timber for shelter frame construction.

Taking refuge in the branches with a Tarzan-type tree hut has a romantic appeal. In reality, however, trees are constantly moving and bending with the wind. Tree huts are unnecessarily dangerous. Using a tree trunk as a centre pole for your shelter may also seem like a good idea. Remember, though, that tree trunks move in windy conditions, and when it rains, water flows down the trunk to the ground. However, heavy snow on evergreens such as spruce can create excellent havens.

LIGHTNING

Lone trees can be dangerous. Lightning likes to find earth, and often chooses to do this by way of a decent conductor. If there are no buildings, communication masts, wreckage or umbrellas, it will use a tree instead.

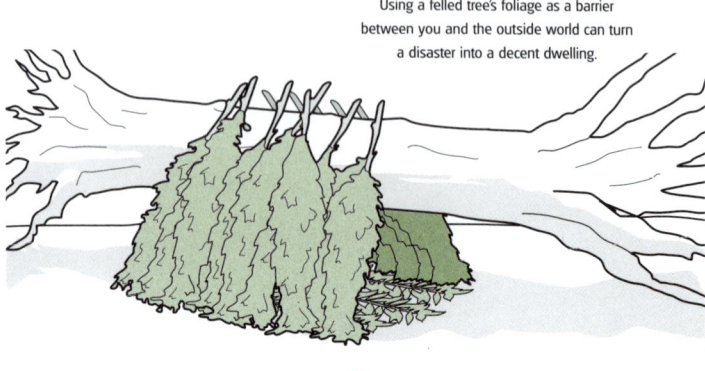

Using a felled tree's foliage as a barrier between you and the outside world can turn a disaster into a decent dwelling.

Shelters and Shelter-Building

You can feel the build-up to an electric storm. The air feels heavier – thicker, even. The sky is likely to contain huge, anvil-shaped clouds called cumulonimbus. In exposed situations, you may also experience a tingling feeling. Once you see a flash of lightning, count the seconds until you hear the thunder. Three seconds equates to one kilometre, so you can work out how far away the lightning is and how long you have to get safe. If you are on an exposed ridge, you need to move down off it, even if the storm is upon you. Lightning strikes come quickly as the storm approaches a mountain, slowing as it passes over. Get into the mountain's lee to reduce the chances of strikes. If you have no decent shelter, it sit or lie in the open on luggage, thick vegetation, a coiled rope or some other insulator. After the storm, felled trees can form a very effective shelter.

JUNGLE SHELTERS

Jungles, like woodlands, offer plenty of materials. Jungles range from lush greenery to large areas of open scrubland. For the most part, the jungle environment consists of a great abundance of competing vegetation. In their natural primary state, jungles have lots of tall, straight trees that rise, pole-like, from the floor for 60 metres or more before their branches spread and interlock with those of neighbouring trees. They form a dense canopy that blocks out sunlight. Little grows below the canopy, so most creatures live up in that, and therefore travel through primary jungle is relatively easy. Unfortunately, humanity has destroyed most primary jungle, as a way of clearing areas that are then farmed. Trees are cut down and the jungle floor exposed to sunlight. When mankind is done with the area, fast-growing vegetation quickly establishes itself, making it virtually impossible for the slow-growing trees to grow back. This secondary jungle becomes very dense. It is home to a great deal of insect and animal life, and difficult to move through.

Shelters will vary depending on the type of jungle you are in. You should always construct a sleeping area off the ground, as millions of jungle insects live in the dead and decaying vegetation on a typical jungle floor. Torrential rain can also flood the ground.

MOORLAND SHELTERS

Moorland consists of peaty soil covered with heather, coarse grasses and moss. There is little cover above knee height, so you need to keep your shelter low to the ground. Peat acts like a sponge, and holds a great deal of water. Once you disturb it – for example, dig into it – the hole soon fills with brown water. Shelter construction in moorland can be very testing, but you

Shelters and Shelter-Building

can protect yourself from the cold, rain and wind by keeping the shelter low, slightly off the ground and comfortably small.

If you have the time and tools, you can construct a decent shelter by cutting blocks of peat to form a tunnel and using local vegetation to form the roof. On higher moorland areas, you can use snow to roof the thatching for insulation.

STURDY SNOW SHELTERS

Most people understand the concept of using snow to form an igloo. The snow used is very compacted, and cut using a long saw/knife. If the snow is of the right texture, and you have the means and the time to cut it and can stand hard work, you can make a very comfortable shelter.

No matter what type of snow shelter you construct, you will find the task difficult and physically demanding. Digging and cutting tools certainly help. However, it is possible to construct a basic shelter using just hands.

A firm drift of snow – or a slope – makes construction easier, as you can burrow into it. Keep your shelter small so you do not lose heat once inside.

The entrance should be as small as possible, with just enough room to squeeze in and out.

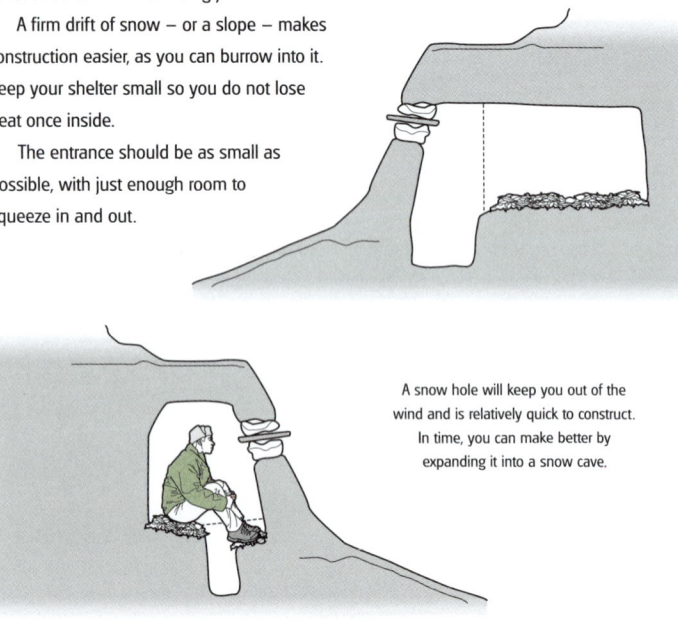

A snow hole will keep you out of the wind and is relatively quick to construct. In time, you can make better by expanding it into a snow cave.

Shelters and Shelter-Building

A small opening is much easier to seal from the inside, keeping weather out. Snow is a good insulator, and will keep the wind off; in fact, the temperature inside a well-constructed snow shelter can be many degrees higher than outside. Heat rises, and cool air falls, so construct a shelf to sit or lie on, with a cold air trough well below. You will have to insulate yourself from the snow you lie on by using any vegetation or extra clothing you can find. The trough will also act as a drain. Body heat in snow shelters melts a thin layer of snow. By building a dome, the melt water runs down the inside walls, stopping drips. It then collects in the trough and freezes. If there is a persistent drip, pushing snow on to it will stop it.

EMERGENCY SNOW SHELTERS

On deep, flat snow you may have to resort to a trench – it's not as effective as a snow cave, but it will get you out of the wind quickly. The roof is the main problem.

If you can cut slabs of snow or ice, you can use these to construct a pitched roof. Branches from trees are good, if present. Pack the frame with snow to further insulate and seal it, but ensure that the frame can support the weight. If you are forced to stay in it, expand it to a cave.

In areas of loose, shallow snow, you should roll up three giant snowballs and push them together. Heap soft snow over them to form a mound. The mound will soon consolidate, and then you can burrow into it to form a decent shelter.

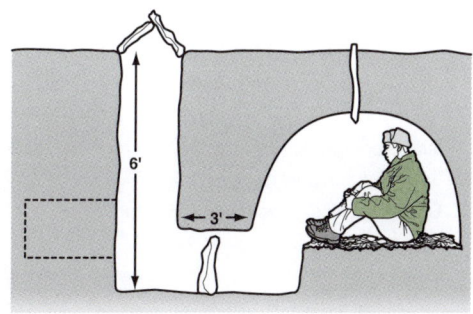

A simple snow trench (above, right) may be the only shelter you need in an emergency. As you consolidate your position, you can improve on the basic design.

Shelters and Shelter-Building

DESERT SHELTERS

A desert is a region devoid (or virtually devoid) of vegetation, usually because of a lack of free water. Deserts form one-fifth of the Earth's surface. The largest areas surround the Persian Gulf and the Red Sea. Saudi Arabia holds the majority of the largest sand desert in the world, the Rub al-Khali (the Empty Quarter). Covering some 250,000 square kilometres, this naked land is awesome. Like all great sand deserts, there are enormous dunes hundreds of metres high. These mammoth features move metres every day, and are capable of engulfing whole cities. Despite its hostility, mankind can and does live in this challenging environment.

In a survival situation, it is generally better to stay in one place and to make the most of the resources you can find locally. Movement on foot is difficult and dangerous. Desert sand is hard, sharp and angular, not like beach sand. It is best to rest by day in a large shelter constructed to offer as much shade as possible, with a flow of fresh air. At night, the shelter should be closed down tightly and made as small as possible to conserve heat, as night-time temperatures often drop well below freezing. Broken-down or wrecked vehicles may seem like good shelter, but become burningly hot by day and lethally freezing at night. Seeking shade under the vehicle is also dangerous, as the weight often makes it sink in soft sand.

Sand is difficult to build shelters from. Tunnelling is dangerous; a scrape or hollow is safer. A piece of wreckage can be used as a roof. Covering it over with sand helps to insulate it slightly.

GENERAL SHELTER-BUILDING

Position will significantly affect your shelter's effectiveness. You may not have the chance to choose a site properly. However, once the initial trauma is over, you should make an effort to improve your shelter and make it a more comfortable and weatherproof. The following pointers apply for most shelters and shelter-building techniques.

- ▲ **If at all possible, get down to a lower level. Avoid exposed ridges**
- ▲ **Select a site on level ground**
- ▲ **Clear the ground of debris and loose rocks**
- ▲ **Keep off damp ground**
- ▲ **Keep away from lone trees and any other lightning-attractor**
- ▲ **Ensure you will not be exposed to falling rocks, branches, and other hazards**

Shelters and Shelter-Building

- ▲ Keep away from dead and rotting vegetation and other features that harbour insects and their nests
- ▲ Constructing a shelter close to water (especially swamps and marshes) exposes you to biting insects; it's better to walk a little way to get your water
- ▲ Do not site your shelter in a dry gully; these can flood at any time without warning
- ▲ Get out of the prevailing wind
- ▲ Use strong, fresh, supple timber as the shelter's main frame
- ▲ Pay attention to weatherproofing
- ▲ In cold climates, keep your shelter small to conserve heat, and in hot climates make it large for shade and draughts, but closable at night
- ▲ A small shelter is quicker to construct, uses fewer materials and is easier to keep warm
- ▲ Always ensure there is plenty of fresh air, especially with snow shelters
- ▲ Make sure that your shelter is well marked, and can be seen from the air at long distance – unless you are hiding
- ▲ Construct an entrance that is easy to close, yet large enough to be able to get in and out of quickly in an emergency
- ▲ Insulate the ground well – the more the better. Ground saps body heat very quickly.

Cold Climates

The will to survive meets its sternest test in freezing conditions. These generate an enormous amount of stress that constantly tests the mind and body; problems that normally mean nothing become massive.

Survivors often experience feelings of isolation and deep depression, resulting in great mood swings that undermine efficiency, even in groups, which may become dangerously divided. A sense of humour is a very important tool in all survival situations, but in the cold it is absolutely vital to maintain a sense of camaraderie and positive thought.

The body's adaptability is the survivor's greatest tool. After acclimatization, the survivor copes better with cold and harsh conditions. Protection is the first survival priority; in cold climates, this gives the survivor vital time to begin to acclimatize. In time, the body can even produce extra fat for protective layers. Keeping as warm as possible is therefore vital.

HEAT LOSS

The body fights cold by producing heat, which it does by converting food into heat energy. The more food, the more the heat increases. This heat is transported to the organs and muscles by blood. In extreme cold, keeping moving forces the blood into the body's extremities, reducing the risk of frostbite.

As air cools the outer body, it sends a signal to the brain. The brain – to avoid cooling the body's organs – cuts off circulation to extremities and keeps blood away from the skin. Hands and feet become starved of blood and cool rapidly. Lessen this effect by keeping as much of the body as possible covered to preserve body heat.

The body responds to cooling by shivering to generate heat. Shivering does help, but it is not constant – nor is it the same for everyone. Some people will continually shiver for long periods, while others will shiver in short bursts. Nevertheless, shivering uses muscles, muscles need blood to operate and blood brings warmth. Obviously, when we use muscles we increase the need for energy, so shivering requires food.

Surviving Cold, Wet Conditions

Cold conditions can be dry or wet. Cold and dry is bad enough, but when you add water, the survival encounter becomes a whole lot worse.

You lose body heat much more quickly when wet, so the body has to work a lot harder. You can become wet three ways: water from rain or watercourses, from snow and ice as it melts, and from the body's sweat. Working physically to survive in cold regions while trying to keep warm often means that you have to work fully clothed. Sweat permeates the clothing and the body heat melts snow and ice. The result is a lot of water held in your clothing.

Whenever possible, remove or add layers of clothing to regulate your body heat while working. If you have a change of warm, dry clothing, keep this in your shelter to wear at rest. If not, try to dry your clothing at every opportunity; a fire is the ideal drying medium, but may not be possible. In some areas, it is possible to hang clothing outside, let it freeze and then knock ice crystals off by beating it with a stick. This crude freeze-dry method will not fully dry your clothes, but if carried out regularly it will get rid of excessive water.

You will have to get used to damp clothing, though. You may need to put spare clothing on top of your wet clothes. There have been many debates in survival training circles about the merits of this. The priority is to keep as warm as possible to prevent hypothermia and the organ starvation it brings, exposure (chilling of the body surface, reducing body temperature) and exhaustion, which also saps body heat. You can only do this by reducing heat loss, which is best achieved by adding clothing. This gives you a better chance of trapping body heat between the layers. The clothing should not be tight, otherwise it will restrict circulation. If you have companions, huddle as closely together as possible to share body heat.

PRIMARY COLD, WET WEATHER RISKS

Damp and wetness are major hazards. Wherever possible, keep out of the rain and snow. Putting insulation – spruce boughs or some other thick padding – between you and the ground will also reduce the thawing from the body being in contact with snow and ice.

When it stays constantly wet from sweat, rain or melt-water, skin becomes saturated. It gets very prone to injury, and sores break out; they can easily become infected. Footwear loses protective properties with long exposure to water and ice too. Blisters on heels and toes often go unnoticed due to numbing from the cold. Frostbite takes hold very quickly and must be prevented at all costs, so check feet and legs regularly for cuts or scrapes.

Wind chill is also much more dangerous when the body is wet. In a survival situation, you must understand the relationship between wind chill, cold and wetness. These three components together account for many deaths.

WIND CHILL

When considering a shelter in cold, wet conditions, you should first establish the prevailing wind direction, and shelter from it. This is not necessarily the way the current wind is blowing, so be careful. You can use local signs to work out the usual direction: for example, trees will grow bending away from the prevailing wind, and a row of tall bushes will show stunted growth on the side from which the wind usually blows.

The speed of the wind is even more important, as that determines wind chill. In 1883, a British naval hydrographer, Admiral Sir Francis Beaufort, devised a scale of wind speed which was adopted by the Admiralty. It is now internationally recognized as the Beaufort Scale.

The mean air temperature in your location may be well above the level of danger from freezing to death. The wind speed can quickly take you below the danger point, however, even in supposedly temperate areas.

Surviving in Hot Conditions

In hot conditions, the main danger is the sun and its heat. Sunlight is an extremely dangerous force that is often overlooked until the damage is done. It is far easier to avoid the sun than to fix the damage it does.

Always keep as much of your body as possible covered in loose, thin layers of clothing. This protects from the sun's rays, and also traps sand and dust, allowing cooler air to reach the skin. Constant sun-glare can damage the eyes, too. If you have sunglasses or goggles, keep them on. If not, make a pair of shades by cutting card, material, bark, or some other medium to fit, and look through thin slits to cut down on the glare.

In sandy deserts, wear a face-cloth to protect you from wind-blown sand. Small sandstorms known as sand devils whip up and can engulf you in an instant. Keep your eyes and mouth closed, and use a cloth to filter out the dust while breathing through your nose. Also avoid walking or resting in dried riverbeds. These wadis can and do flash-flood without warning, no matter how unlikely it seems at the time.

SALT LOSS

In hot climates, you will sweat a great deal. Sweating reduces core body temperature through evaporation. As we sweat, we lose body fluids, so drinking plenty is critical. But we also lose essential minerals including salt, carried out on the sweat; drinking water alone will not replace these. Extreme salt loss can kill as quickly as excessive salt intake.

Evaporating water from the sea can yield some salt, although it is highly inefficient; seawater only has 3%. The best source is food, such as locally-caught game and fish Hot climates lessen your appetite, but you must fight this and continue to eat normally. Minimise sweating by moving and working during the cooler parts of the day and night.

Heat quickly saps energy and motivation. It can be hard to tackle even the simplest tasks. The lack of proper diet and water will drag morale down, testing your will to survive to its limits. Heat also pushes the body to extremes. In hot deserts, sand and dust cling to sweat, causing sores and blisters which must be dealt with immediately. In the tropics, constant wetness makes the skin break easily, and wounds quickly become infected and infested with horrible parasites. Keep as cool and as clean as possible.

Surviving Water

Most of the Earth's surface is covered in seawater, and there are millions of rivers and lakes. Your survival encounter is probably going to involve navigating expanses of water, or at least negotiating a significant river.

Water is actually a very hostile and harsh environment. It has no hiding place from the weather, it is constantly moving and it is inherently inimical to human life. Salt water is not even drinkable. Before you decide to negotiate flowing waters, take time to properly assess the best position to cross. On large, open bodies of water, be aware of the effect the wind will have on you and any craft you use.

CAPSIZING

Many people survive water with a raft or dinghy. You are most likely to be in an open-water situation because of a mishap such as a shipwreck, a small boat capsizing or a dinghy being blown away from a holiday beach. Being able to right a capsized boat is one of the fundamental skills in water survival.

If a capsize does happen, the first thing to remember is not to lose contact with your craft. Keep hold and hang on until you can reorganize your wits. If you have a sailboat, you must manoeuvre the boat so that your back is to the prevailing wind, at the rear of your craft. If there are two or more of you, then one person needs to be at the front, in a position to be scooped up when the boat is righted. The rest, if any, should help righting the boat. You then climb on the daggerboard – keep as close as possible to the hull to avoid excess pressure – or if there isn't one, grab the boat at the rail where the hull meets the far side deck. Place your feet on the hull and lean back to use your weight to right the boat. It will leave the water slowly at first, but once the sail clears the water the process becomes much easier.

AIRCRAFT DINGHIES

If you are a passenger in an aircraft that has had to ditch in the sea, you should have one of the inflatable dinghies that planes stow for this eventuality, along with a regulation inflatable life jacket. Once on the dinghy, get away from the aircraft in case it explodes or

Surviving Water

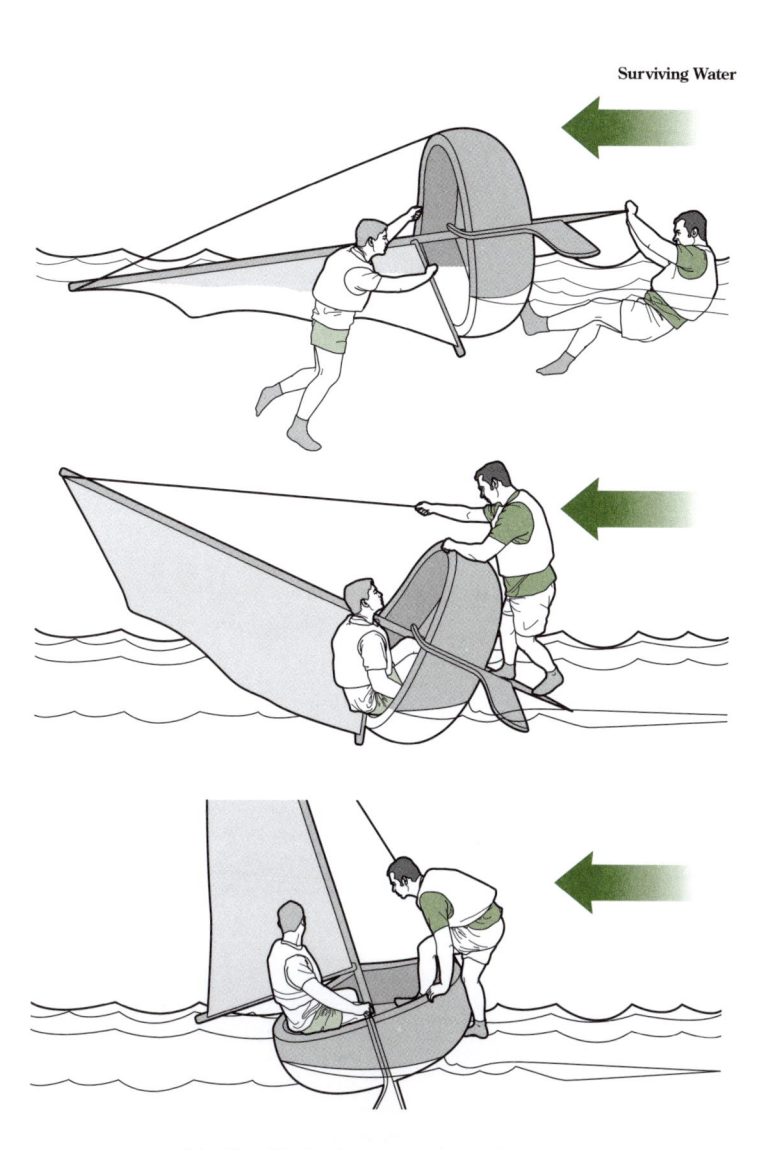

Being able to right a boat in an emergency is a simple technique.

Surviving Water

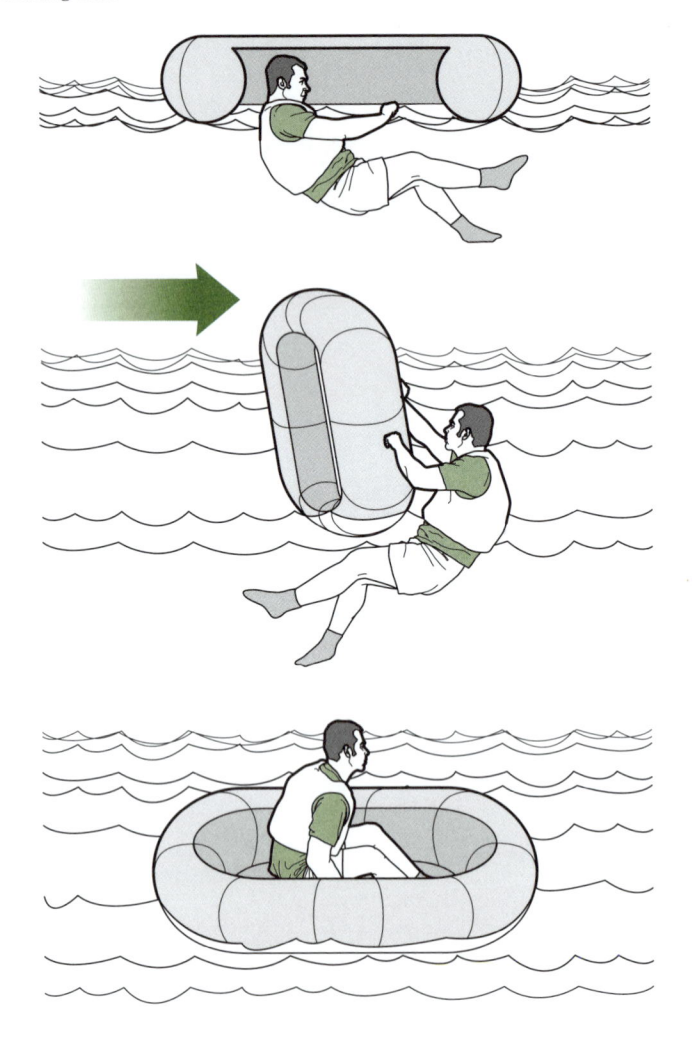

Inverted boats, canoes and dinghies will have an air pocket so you can breathe until you can swim clear. Lift a corner of an inflatable to catch the wind when righting the craft.

Surviving Water

quickly sinks, sucking you under with it. Fix any damage to the craft as soon as possible; there is usually a repair kit stowed in an inner pocket. Then attend to any first aid requirements. Where possible, protect against cold by putting extra clothes on or sharing body heat. If there are other survival craft in the area, join up with them and tie all the floating craft together. As soon as possible, prepare your signalling equipment and make it ready for use. Stores and food may well be floating around the crash site; collect as much as possible without endangering yourself or others.

Protection from the weather is the next consideration. You may have a dinghy with a hood; if so, fasten it tightly, but if not, try to construct a roof from spare clothing or anything else. There may be fresh water in the craft, or it may have a solar still system. If not, set up waterproof clothing to catch rainwater. You may need to ration water until you can properly assess the situation. There might be food that also needs rationing, or you may have to fish. If there are any survival pamphlets aboard, read and follow them. Finally, make a shift plan that ensures one person is always ready with flares or other signals, and another is awake to sail the craft.

RIGHTING INFLATABLE CRAFT

Inflatable craft are light, and can easily end up inverted on launch. If so, swim around the craft so that the wind blows in your face. Then use your weight to push down on the craft so that the far edge leaves the water. The wind will get under it and flip it over, so remember to keep hold. Once the craft is up, swim around so that the wind is blowing from behind you before boarding. As soon as you are safely aboard, bail out any water inside and follow the procedures outlined above.

TIDES AND CURRENTS

Tides rise and fall approximately every 12 hours according to sun and moon. Their greatest strength is when the earth, sun and moon are in line, every 14 days or so. These 'spring' tides can be very high. It takes six hours from high tide to low tide, and the pull is much stronger around the three- to four-hour points. You can only be swept out to sea when the tide is going out. Understanding the relationship between tides, wind and currents can help you to steer your craft.

If you have a sail that you can adjust, the wind should provide the boat's propulsion and navigation. However, if the sail is fixed (or you have none) then your ability to steer is

Surviving Water

restricted. Keeping a watch on the tides, currents and wind may help you to set a course.

In essence, if you stay very low in the craft, keep any sails down and collapse your shelter or cover, the wind is less likely to determine your course; the currents and tides will have the advantage. So if you are in sight of land and the wind is blowing you off course, you can lower the craft's wind resistance and use the currents and inbound tide to pull you in and make a landfall. Or if the wind can assist you, construct a sail or sit high in the craft to catch the wind and use it to push you in.

SWIMMING AND SWIMMERS

If you are forced to make a long swim for safety, leave your clothing on and swim slowly to conserve energy. The swim will be much easier with some form of buoyancy aid. If you cannot see land or do not swim well, hang on tight to any floating wreckage until help arrives.

If you see someone in trouble in the water, summon help before anything. Wherever possible, stay out of the water yourself and throw a line, offer a long pole or make a human chain. If you are a very strong swimmer, you may try a rescue from the water. Do not dive into the water, but enter it slowly. Keep away from the victim and throw clothing or a short line for them to hold; then haul them to safety. If you have absolutely no other alternative, approach the person from behind, talking to them constantly to calm them. A drowning person's reflex urge is to cling to you so tightly that you are both drowned. Many would-be rescuers die that way.

CROSSING RIVERS

Fast-flowing water – rivers and floodwater – should be avoided unless there really is no alternative. Ideally, wait until levels drop. Unfortunately, in survival situations time is often of the essence, and you may have no choice. Never try to hop from boulder to boulder. Wet rocks are slippery, and fallen trees move and roll if stood on. If the water is shallow enough to wade, keep your footwear on. Cross at a spot where the flow is mildest, and avoid submerged trees and other hazards.

Never balance on submerged rocks; probe the riverbed with your feet until you can place your foot fully flat. Do not over-stretch. Even the mildest of currents can unbalance you easily. Once in the water, watch upstream carefully for debris that may be a hazard. Move slightly into the flow on a diagonal course. If you have a pack, hold it by one strap over the downstream arm and be ready to let it go if you get into any trouble. Face the bank to lessen resistance.

Move one leg first and then bring the other to it; crossing your legs will throw out your balance. A stout staff, grounded upstream, makes a good third leg, probe and depth gauge. Attach as many flotation aids as possible to your arms; empty containers and air-filled plastic bags are ideal.

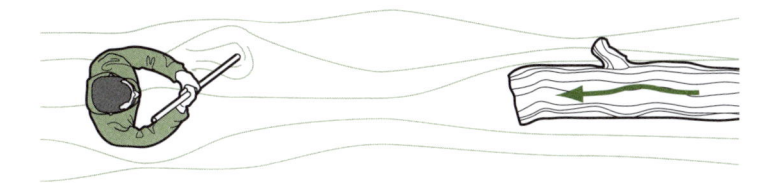

GROUP RIVER CROSSINGS

A group can safely cross a river with the use of a rope circle. The strongest member holds the middle of a rope and crosses as below. Assistants hold the rope out just tight, upstream and downstream, closing as the leader crosses. Once across, members use the rope one by one as a safety line. The last person crosses in the same way as the first. If anyone stumbles, the two anchormen act as guide, moving downstream with the fallen person. Standing fast and trying to haul in the fallen person will force the victim under water, while moving at the same speed as the current will automatically guide the victim back to the bank.

If you don't have a rope, you can move a group, if the water is not too deep, by interlocking arms, forming a circle and moving slowly together. In faster water, it can be safer to line up

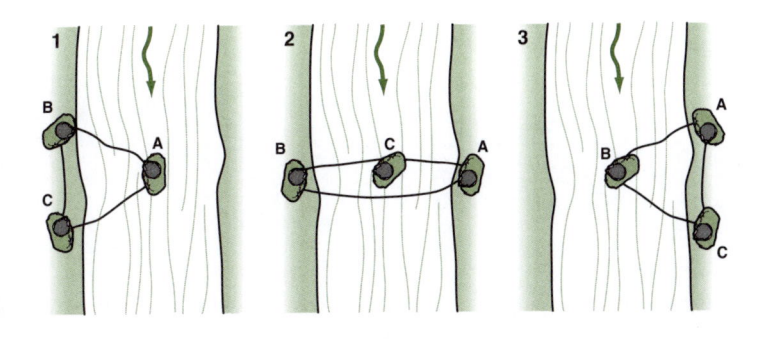

Surviving Water

behind each other in small groups, firmly holding the person in front and moving as described above. The strongest members should be front and rear.

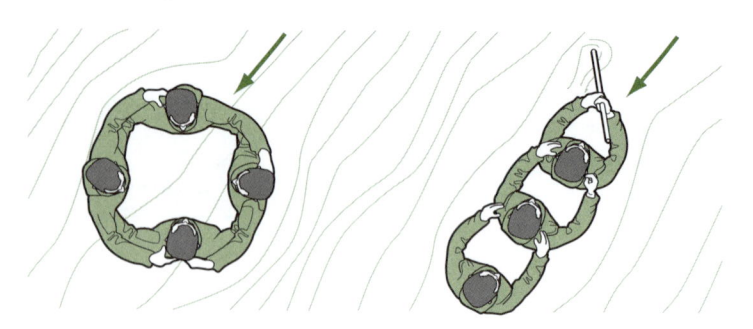

Unless vital, avoid crossing water. If you have no choice, take the time to plan your route across properly.

SURVIVING FLOODS

If you are caught in floods, head quickly for high ground. If not possible, sturdy rooftops are much safer than trees, because the soil can waterlog and weaken roots' grip. If the tree is washed away, you will probably be tangled in its branches and unable to help yourself. If you have no alternative but to climb a tree, plan how to get out of it.

If you get swept away, adopt a sitting position pointing your legs downstream. Keep looking forward, and use your arms to steer away from debris if possible. Keep your feet high in front of you, so you can soften the impact of any solid object you may be forced into.

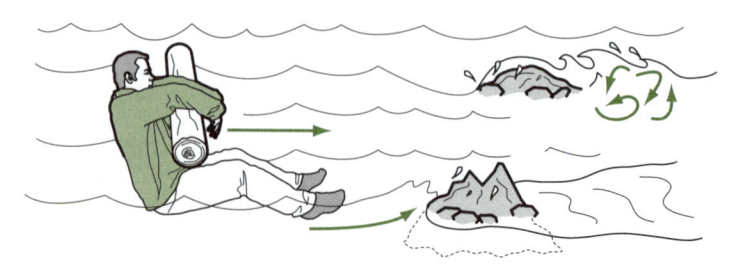

If you are swept away, pick a spot on a downstream bank some distance away and slowly ferry-glide across.

You can also read the water ahead; for example, a sudden swell (especially with a back eddy) indicates a hidden danger under the surface, while rocky outcrops can have relatively calm areas behind them. If you are caught in an eddy or below a weir or waterfall, you can escape by diving below the surface and using the water's natural force to push you out.

DROWN-PROOFING

Whenever you can anticipate water hazards, take the time to find or make floating aids. Floating timber works, or you can tie trousers at the bottoms, filled with fresh air and held tight at the top — normal clothing holds the air better after wetting. Waterproof clothing keeps in the air for much longer.

If you are adrift for long periods, you can conserve heat and energy by carrying out drown-proofing procedures. This involves taking a breath, relaxing, crouching up and then floating just below the surface. Stay like this for as long as you can comfortably, then push down with your arms to force you back to the surface, lift your head out for a breath of air, and repeat.

SURVIVING SWAMPS

Once you approach land, you may have to cross an area of mud or swamp. You can swim over this ground without sinking. Use your clothing, spread in front of you; place your arms, head and chest on top, and make very wide, slow breaststroke actions. Recover your clothing as you pass over it and spread it out in front of you again until you reach solid land.

Swamps can be determined by plant life; tough grasses growing in tussocks, bright green vegetation and reeds are good indicators of waterlogged land. Crossing swamps is extremely hard and slow. If you start to sink, don't panic. Lying down and spreading your body out will slow the sinking long enough for you to breaststroke out to safety. Avoid thrashing around, as this will cause you to sink quickly.

SURVIVING A SUNKEN VEHICLE

Never attempt to cross swollen rivers or flooded areas when driving. Many people die each year trying to drive through floods. They rarely know the depth of the water or the current's force, and the car is quickly swept off and overturned.

If your vehicle enters deep water, quickly get clear before it sinks. If you do not have time, keep the windows fully closed and release your seat-belt. Most cars sink front-first, but a heavy rear load may sink you backwards. Climb away from the sinking end immediately. Once

Surviving Water

the vehicle comes to rest, you will be completely disorientated, but do not panic. With doors and windows shut, the vehicle will not fill up straight away. Air is lighter than water, so water will filter in from the bottom up. The water will be so dirty that you can barely see out, and pressure will make opening the doors impossible.

Grab several deep breaths and, when ready, open a window slowly. As water gushes in, the pressure between the inside and outside will equalize, and opening the doors becomes possible. At the last moment, take a normal deep breath of air and fully open the window so that the vehicle fills. As it does, watch the air bubbles – they are heading for the surface, and you need to follow them to safety. You should now be able to open the doors to escape, but if you can't, the window is open. As you exit, come out head-first, facing the vehicle all the way, as though performing a forward roll on to the roof (or bottom, if the car is upside down). You can bend virtually double from the stomach, but your bending backwards movement is very restricted. You may become stuck if you try to come out normally.

⚠ Surviving Fire

Fire spreads at an alarming rate – especially with enough fuel and oxygen to keep it going. The way to put out a fire is to restrict fuel and starve it of oxygen.

If you are caught up in a fire you should get as far away as possible. Unless you have experience and equipment to extinguish it, leave it alone. If you cannot get out easily, you will have to assess the best way of dealing with the situation.

If you are visiting a building – especially to sleep – then make sure that you can locate its extinguishers easily, and check the way they work. Be absolutely sure, as you will only need them in an emergency, and probably in the dark. Wherever you stay, know the quickest route to safety. Walk and clear emergency exit routes. If you have to put up with inadequate official routes, take the time to work out an alternative route to safety. Know how doors and windows open, and check that they are not locked.

EXTINGUISHERS

Your vehicle, home and workplace should all have fire extinguishers handy. Not all extinguishers are the same; for example, a water-based extinguisher is dangerous on an electrical fire. Always check extinguishers to ensure what they can be used on and how they are operated. Most extinguishers have a limited shelf-life, so they should be checked regularly.

FIRE EXTINGUISHER TIPS

- ▲ Paper, wood and cloth fires can be extinguished using any extinguisher
- ▲ Vehicle fires should be extinguished with foam or powder extinguishers only
- ▲ Foam, CO2 gas and powder should be used on flammable liquids, not water
- ▲ Gas and electric fires must be extinguished using CO2 or powder and, if possible, disconnect the supply

When properly maintained, smoke alarms are the most effective fire warning. Fit them everywhere you stay. Visiting locations with smoke alarms, check that they are working properly; if this proves difficult, ask to see the maintenance schedule. Do not assume that they are working simply because they are fitted.

Surviving Fire

VEHICLE FIRE

If a fire breaks out in your car, it will most commonly be in the engine compartment. Electrical fires can start behind the dashboard, usually indicated by a strong smell of melting wiring sleeves. If you ever smell burning – or see wide smoke trails behind your moving car – pull over and check the vehicle thoroughly. If smoke is billowing out from under the bonnet, do not open it; you'll allow more oxygen in, and the flames will leap out and could seriously burn you. Once certain a fire is present, move away and alert the emergency services.

Do not go back into the vehicle to retrieve anything. The vehicle may explode without warning.

Aircraft can catch fire from impact, wiring shorts or engine fault. Pilots can deal with engine fire effectively, as modern aeroplane engines have a fire extinguisher system operated from the flight deck. Inside, cabin crew are trained to deal with fire. If fire does take hold, the cabin can fill with dense, black smoke. Drop down to the floor to get some air. Once the plane is down, stay at floor level. Look for the illuminated floor-level strips to indicate the way to the nearest exit, and follow them.

BUILDING FIRE

Panic and fear lead to poor decision-making. If you are confronted with fire and smoke, keep calm and logically work your way out of the situation.

If smoke is filtering through the cracks around a room door, do not open it. Put the bck of your hand close to the door. If the fire is outside, you will feel the heat. If you cannot feel any heat, gently touch the door with the back of your hand, ready to pull it away quickly to lessen burns. If it is cool to the touch, carefully open the door and follow your emergency exit route. If it is hot, assume the fire is outside. Keep the door closed, using wet bedding or any other material to plug the gaps, then move to a window and either escape or attract attention to yourself.

If you can leave the room but not the building, move to a room as low down and as far from the fire as possible. Do not go higher. If it is possible to jump without injury or you have a rope, or enough material to manufacture one, then either abseil down or use the building-escape technique (see page 65).

It is safer to land where the ground is soft, and you may be able to cushion your landing area by first throwing out bedding and other soft furnishings.

Surviving Fire

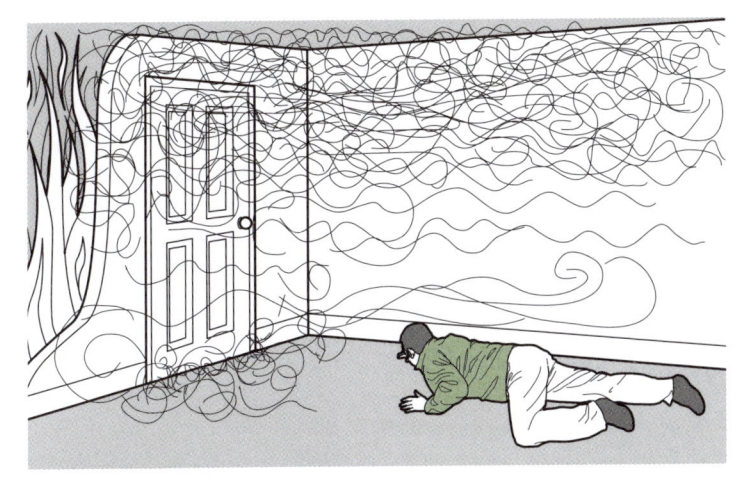

Before opening, carefully feel any door – if it is hot, the fire is on the other side; do not open!

OUTDOOR FIRES

Fires in the open are usually easier to escape from than building fires, but you must act decisively to escape. Basically, the wind determines the direction and speed of the fire. If you are in a forest, follow the wildlife, which will be moving away. In managed woodland, wide paths called firebreaks should halt a fire; cross as many as possible. If you are completely cut off and can find a pool or stream, submerge in it and use a hollow reed or wooden tube as a breathing pipe. If there is a fast-flowing river, you may be forced to jump into it and use it to float you away. This is highly dangerous, and only you can make the decision to go to this extreme.

Street Survival

Street crime is a global constant. There are many reasons, but the most important question is how criminals choose victims in the first place. Is it just a case of being in the wrong place at the wrong time? If so – and evidence suggests this – then the survivor has to be in the right place at the right time. This means taking precautions to avoid attack by reducing our profile as a target, and thinking about crimes against the person and how to avoid them.

Most people feel safe in their local environment; there is still a risk of crime but you know how to manage it, by avoiding certain places or people. The problem most often comes when you move away from the areas you know. No army would enter battle without knowing the location they were deploying in, yet many people travel around the world without any background knowledge of the areas they will visit. Before embarking on any trip, you should take time to learn about the place and people. If there are dangerous areas, you need to know so that you can avoid them, or at least ascertain safest times or how to arrange an escort.

Theft is the second oldest profession in the world. If you walk around with a bag of money on show, someone will go for it. Unless they are desperate, the chances are that they will wait until you are in an isolated place, or at a location offering easy escape.

STREET CRIME MANAGEMENT

You can reduce the risk of street crime by avoiding places that you know are potential trouble-spots. Keep away from dangerous neighbourhoods. If you aren't sure, ask the local police, the tourist information centre or the owners of the hotel in which you are staying. When out and about, think as the criminal does; you are safer in a busy, well-lit street than a back street with fewer people and poor lighting. When possible, cross intersections on the surface and avoid underpasses. If there is no alternative, wait until you can walk through with a group of people. If you are going to a meeting or friend's apartment, make appointments early in the day to avoid leaving premises late. This is especially important if the places you are visiting are isolated office blocks or industrial units, or are located out of town. The local area may be very busy when you arrive, but after normal working

Street Survival

hours the chances are that the whole area becomes quiet, dark and more dangerous.

In all cases, criminals hunting outside their own community look for opportunity. The best opportunities are found when targets are out of their usual environment and packed together – such as bad districts that offer handy shortcuts, shopping areas that attract out-of-towners and tourist areas and resorts. A second set of hotel door or hire car keys may be available for a share of the take, and some criminals haunt bars and discos for the right target – usually some unsuspecting mark who has been flashing money around, clearly the worse for drink.

SURVIVING BEING TAILED

In unfamiliar territory, the best policy is to stick to members-only bars and clubs situated on main city streets. Some members-only clubs allow anyone in on payment of a joining fee, so watch this. Even so, criminals may mark you as a target. Control your drinking, and watch for any unusual bar staff activity. Be aware of your surroundings; if you feel uneasy, trust your feelings and leave, making sure you have a taxi waiting for you.

If you suspect you are being followed, quicken your pace a bit. If you do not gain distance, it may indicate that the other person has sped up too. If there are open shops, go into one and wait for the person to go by.

Alternatively, ask a shopkeeper or passer-by the way to the local police station; it may be very close, in which case you can walk there quickly. If you are still unsure, try crossing the street. If the person also crosses, then you have to assume you are in danger; pick someone specific nearby and ask that person for help. Do not leave the main streets, walk into a deadend or try to take a shortcut.

MINIMIZING RISKS

Before journeying in an area you don't know, make sure you memorise the exact route. Most towns and cities have decent street atlases. Buy one and study it; looking out for prominent features such as police stations and hospitals. Ask hotel staff or someone you can trust to mark high crime areas and other risky places on the maps. If there are no maps, use an official taxi.

Think about the most sensible clothing to wear. Provocative clothing can be dangerous, and tight pockets show purses and wallets clearly. Never carry cash or cards in hand. Even when nervous, look confident. Looking unsure or lost is a sure way to attract criminal attention. Stay alert, and always stand and act as though you are totally in control of yourself and your surroundings. Keep low-denomination notes in one pocket, medium-denomination in another and high-value notes in a third

Street Survival

to avoid flashing cash. If the currency is unfamiliar, take your time paying. If you have to go to a cash machine or local bank, carry out your transaction keeping close to the machine or counter to stop anyone from seeing your personal identification number or the amount of cash you have withdrawn.

Tips to Avoid Street Crime

- ▲ Walk and act with absolute confidence; even when you're lost, act as though you belong
- ▲ Keep your camera, shopping bags and handbags close to and in front of your body; if you carry a bag with a strap, wear it with the strap across your body
- ▲ Walk facing the oncoming traffic to avoid a car pulling up behind you and snatching your belongings
- ▲ Avoid walking close to doorways and entrances, where someone may be lurking
- ▲ Do not drink so much alcohol that you lose control
- ▲ Keep to well-lit streets and main highways
- ▲ Wear clothing that is practical and not provocative; loose clothing with many pockets allows you to carry valuables discreetly. To really blend in, wear clothing bought from a local second-hand or thrift store
- ▲ Keep away from known trouble-spots
- ▲ Avoid gangs of youngsters
- ▲ Make sure that you know the political, religious and racial feeling of the area
- ▲ Keep well away from derelict buildings, open, deserted land, parkland and isolated office and industrial units
- ▲ Stay with the majority of the local people; avoid becoming isolated and alone
- ▲ Do not stop if asked for directions or engaged in any sort of conversation; keep walking as if you haven't heard
- ▲ Use properly licensed taxicabs and other transport
- ▲ Carry a personal attack alarm, a flashlight and a whistle
- ▲ If you think you are being followed, make your way directly to a police station, call for assistance or seek refuge in a local shop or private dwelling.

⚠ Self-Defence

By far the best defence is to avoid getting into a violent situation in the first place. When violence seems imminent, leave if possible. If not, try to negotiate. If being robbed, give up your goods without protest. Do not die for a camcorder or credit card. Never underestimate the power of speech; if you can reason with the aggressor and defuse the situation, then you have achieved the ultimate goal – stopping yourself or others being injured or killed.

If you can see that an area is unsafe or that a particular group of people have violent tendencies (or weapons), do not get involved with them. When travelling – especially in unfamiliar territory – stay vigilant for escape routes and safe places.

It is a fact of life that people will and do resort to physical violence. The problem is that you cannot always tell who is dangerous and who is not. Be wary of everyone you do not know well, and expect the unexpected. This advice is particularly true when you are unsure about the place you are visiting or the local customs and practices.

FIGHTING BACK

When there is no alternative, and you are faced with violence against yourself or loved ones, you have to fight back. Fight very aggressively, and aim to completely stop the aggressor physically. You may not be naturally aggressive, but you can still overwhelm a heavier, more experienced combatant. Start with intense confidence, and the aggressor may give up immediately. Most bullies are cowards, and choose targets on the basis of intimidation. Show them you are not a pushover, and you create an advantage.

Caution

Never, ever practise the moves in this book on a real person, even just part-way. You may murder a friend if you do. Use bags and training dummies.

Self-Defence

There are thousands of fighting and self-defence techniques. I like Tae Kwon Do, but you must spar regularly against other fighters to keep any edge, so I believe non-fighters should concentrate on a small number of proven techniques that are easy to master and remember in a crisis. When you do practise fighting techniques, wear your usual clothing and footwear. Learning to fight wearing special training clothing is not realistic; you will be surprised how different the moves feel in non-optimal clothing.

When an attack happens, do not expect warning. An attack will come in an instant. If you have not prepared the situation, you will be taken before you can get ready.

Keeping your balance and being able to lessen impact are critical. Before being attacked, move into a defence position. Don't just square off at any hint of verbal aggression, though; that may start an avoidable fight. Moving into defensive stance without letting the aggressor know gives you a psychological edge, and leaves you ready if the confrontation escalates. Of course, if assaulted without verbal indication, you should snap into defensive stance straight away.

Basic Defence Stance

The basic non-fighter's defence stance can be adopted quickly if jumped, or slowly entered subtly.

Firstly, turn your body to point your left shoulder at the aggressor. Position your feet firmly on the ground, pointing your left foot at him, and slightly bend the left knee. Slide the right leg back with the foot at a right-angle to the lead foot, using it as a stabilizer; keeping the knee locked, you will have a very solid stance. If attacked, you have reduced the attacker's target area. From here, you can quickly go to the full defence stance by quickly lifting your lead shoulder and tucking your chin behind it, pointing your forehead at the attacker. Keep your mouth shut to avoid a broken jaw. Lift your right hand up to cover the exposed side of your face, and drop your left hand down to defend against a kick to the groin. Lean back so that your head is out of the aggressor's reach, and be ready to fend off the initial attack, then counter-attack or run.

Be ready for an initial attack, and always look for an escape route. The description shows the stance for a right-handed person. If you are left-handed, simply start with the right shoulder and adjust the rest accordingly.

The Basics

HEAD

When close to your aggressor, use your head to take him off balance by thumping it into his face. This is particularly effective as distraction while performing other techniques, such as disarming him. From about a half a metre in front of him, lunge forward, pushing off your back foot forcefully, and flick your head forward to hit him full in the face. Use as much force as possible; aim for the bridge of the aggressor's nose with the bony top of your high forehead. Avoid bending backwards first, as this gives warning.

TEETH

If you are being held close, bite into the aggressor's flesh. Try to bite right through so your teeth meet. A bite is excruciatingly painful, and even the most hardened aggressor will let go, especially if you are biting through ear or fingers.

CLENCHED FIST

A punch is delivered with fist tightly closed and the thumb outside the fingers; the wrist should be rigid, not bent. The best point of impact is with the first and second knuckles only, as this concentrates the force. Aim for the eyes, nose, lower jaw and just below the cheekbone. A strong blow to the soft area just below the breastbone, where the ribs come together, will wind the aggressor. If you are low enough, a sharp blow to the lower stomach or testicles will bring your aggressor down. To get the optimum force behind your fist, keep your feet firmly planted on the ground and swing your hips to move your upper body around. Hit with the right hand, so you can put your weight and power into the shoulders as they pivot and transmit it down the arm into the punch.

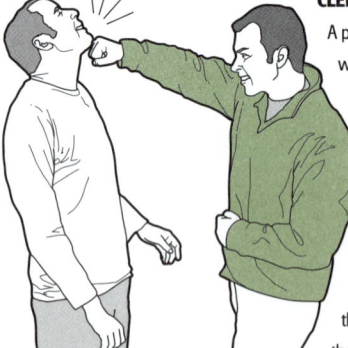

The Basics

EDGE OF THE HAND

The hand should be rigid, with the fingers tightly kept together and straight. The thumb should be extended at a right-angle to the hand. Hit with the fleshy area half-way between the joint of the little finger and the wrist. The technique is to strike from a bent arm, adding power with body weight and extra speed by straightening the arm as you hit. Either chop down, or swing the hand horizontally, keeping the palm face down.

The blow is most effective in the soft flesh around the base of the skull where it meets the neck. A powerful blow across the carotid artery will cut blood to the brain and cause massive bruising – both of which will render the aggressor unconscious. A slicing/swinging blow just under the Adam's apple with sufficient force to flatten the windpipe will kill the attacker. If you are held by your clothing, pull back so the aggressor's arm is straightened and use a chopping blow on to the forearm: this will fracture the forearm bones.

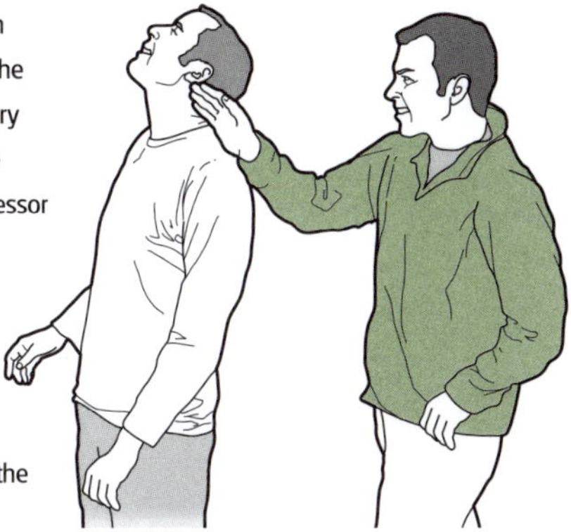

HEEL OF THE HAND

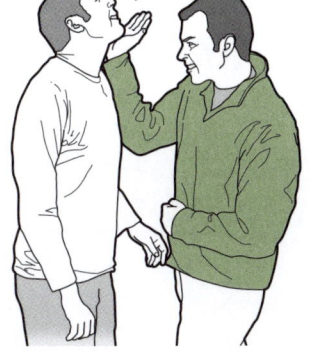

Make a claw shape with the fingers and pull them back, exposing the heel of your hand. From a very close position – around five to six inches (13–16cm) – you should force the heel of your hand up to hit the aggressor under the chin (to knock out) or nose (to possibly kill) with a sharp, powerful blow. If possible, pull him towards the blow by grabbing his shirt. A knee to the groin will also force the aggressor to drop towards the blow, giving it a lot more force.

Practise these techniques on a punchbag or fighting dummy. Do not wait until confronted with violence, as you will not have the confidence to properly deliver the blows

The Basics

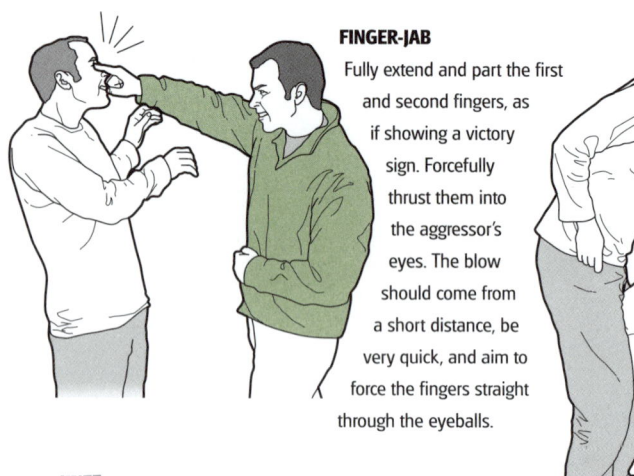

FINGER-JAB

Fully extend and part the first and second fingers, as if showing a victory sign. Forcefully thrust them into the aggressor's eyes. The blow should come from a short distance, be very quick, and aim to force the fingers straight through the eyeballs.

KNEE

The knee should be jerked upwards in a single sharp movement, using the other leg as a stabilizer. Drop your hips as you make impact for extra force. The best area for this blow is the groin. This will bring the aggressor's head down as he bends to try evading the blow, or doubles in pain, so keep your head back. The knee can also target the outside of the upper leg approximately half-way between the knee and the hip. This hits the aggressor's leg nerves and deadens the muscle, causing severe pain. He will have trouble walking for a bit, giving you a chance to escape.

KICKS

There are many ways of delivering an effective kick. Without professional training, the best way is to kick with the leg fully extended, using the front of the shoe as the striking area. A kick allows you a good distance from the aggressor – if you are too close, then there is not enough force to do any real

The Basics

damage. The most effective distance is at the end of a fully stretched leg. The leg muscles are powerful, and can deliver a very strong and powerful blow. Aim for the groin, but if the aggressor is on the floor, aim for his jaw, neck or throat – sometimes a fatal blow.

THE SIDE AND HEEL OF THE FOOT

When held close, use the side and heel of your foot. Lift your leg, place either the inside or outer edge of your foot just below the aggressor's knee and stamp down, scraping your foot down the shin and aiming the heel at the bridge of his foot. As the heel hits, take your other foot off the ground to put your full body weight into the strike. This often breaks his foot, collapsing the bridge, so the aggressor is unable to pursue you if you can run.

A killing blow can be delivered to an aggressor who is down and lying on his back or front. Jump in the air approximately half a metre high, pull the toes back and the front of your foot upwards so that you strike with your heels, and land on the lower chest or middle back. This focuses your weight and power on the organs, causing massive damage and often sudden death to the aggressor.

Vulnerable Parts of the Body

A EYES, EARS, NOSE, CHIN
B NECK/THROAT
C COLLAR BONE
D SOLAR PLEXUS
E LOWER STOMACH
F GROIN
G KNEE
H SHIN
I INSTEP
J CROWN
K BELOW/BEHIND EARS
L BASE OF SKULL
M COCCYS BONE
N KIDNEYS
O KNEE JOINT
P HEEL

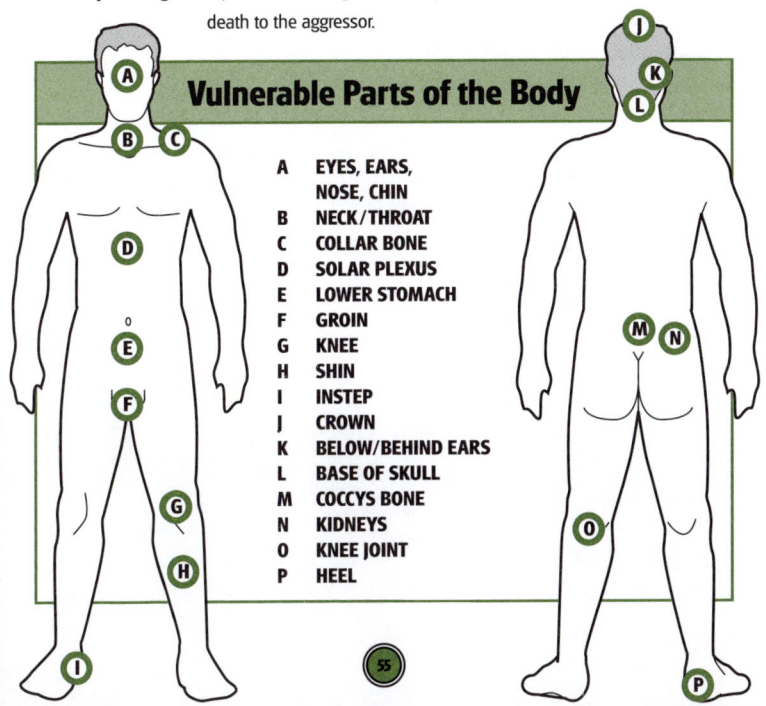

The Basics

KILLING WITH KNIVES

Knives are used to kill. If someone has pulled a knife on you, you must assume he intends murder. Likewise, pulling a knife yourself escalates any fight to lethal status. Only draw a knife when ready to kill. If you are half-hearted, the aggressor will disarm you and turn your knife on you. The best knives have a sharp point and two straight, sharp sides, and are at least 6.5 inches (17cm) long.

If you do use a knife, the fight will be lethally dangerous. Aim to kill the aggressor quickly. The best way is to select fatal target areas. Knives kill by causing blood loss; the greater the bleed, the quicker the death. The body's main arteries are the most effective targets.

Knife attack points

A) RADIAL: 0.5 inches (1cm) below the surface; unconsciousness within 30 seconds and death within three minutes.

B) BRACHIAL: Nearly 1 inch (2cm) below the surface; unconsciousness within 14 seconds and death within two minutes.

C) CAROTID: 1.5 inches (4cm) below the surface; severing it will cause unconsciousness within 5 seconds and death within 12 seconds.

D) SUBCLAVIAN: 2 inches (6cm) below the surface; unconsciousness within two seconds and death within four seconds.

E) HEART: 3.5 inches (9cm) below the surface, behind the ribs; unconsciousness within one second and death within three seconds.

F) STOMACH: 5 inches (12cm) below the surface; the length of time to unconsciousness and death depends on the severity of the cut. If targeting the stomach, a stab-and-rip action causes the maximum amount of damage.

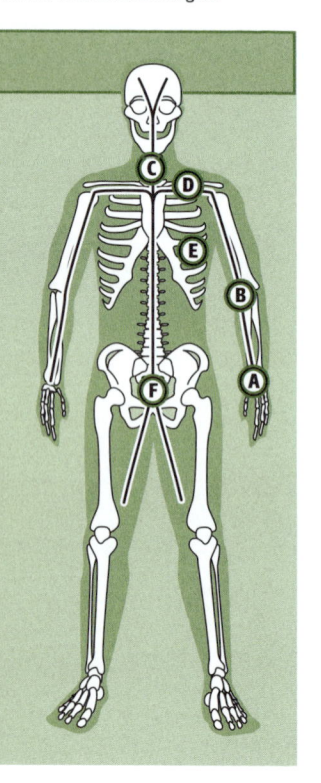

The Basics

ESCAPING THE ONE-HANDED STRANGLEHOLD

If you can break an aggressor's grip, you may be able to run or turn the fight around. One of the simplest release techniques to master is breaking free from a one-hand stranglehold. This is where the aggressor has one hand around your throat to hold you, usually while he hits you. Use the heel of your hand to hit his wrist hard enough to dislodge his hand from your throat while kneeing him sharply in the groin. You weaken his throat grip and, as he realizes that your knee is aimed at his groin, he will pull back, bending his body away from you to try to avoid injury. At this point he will be off-balance, and you can pull away and either run to safety or head-butt him in the face. If your knee landed, you may have injured him enough to permit incapacitation.

ESCAPING THE TWO-HANDED STRANGLEHOLD

With the two-handed stranglehold, the aggressor will be facing you with both hands grabbing you around the throat; his thumbs will be pressed against your windpipe, restricting your breathing. Cross your right hand over the top of his arms and grab his right hand. Push your thumbnail deep into the flesh between his thumb and first finger. At the same time, curl your fingers around his hand and pull the hand away, twisting it as if to sprain the wrist, so that his palm is forced to face upwards.

The Basics

Simultaneously, bring your left hand up to his right elbow – your thumb should go under the elbow and the fingers should hold the back of the elbow, forcing it up to straighten and lock the joint. As he releases his grip and is off-balance, keep a firm hold of him with both hands and turn sharply to your right, twisting the whole of his wrist and arm against the joints. Push down with the elbow grip until he bends forward. You can now deliver a blow to the back of his elbow with the edge of your hand or use your weight to crush the elbow with your left knee.

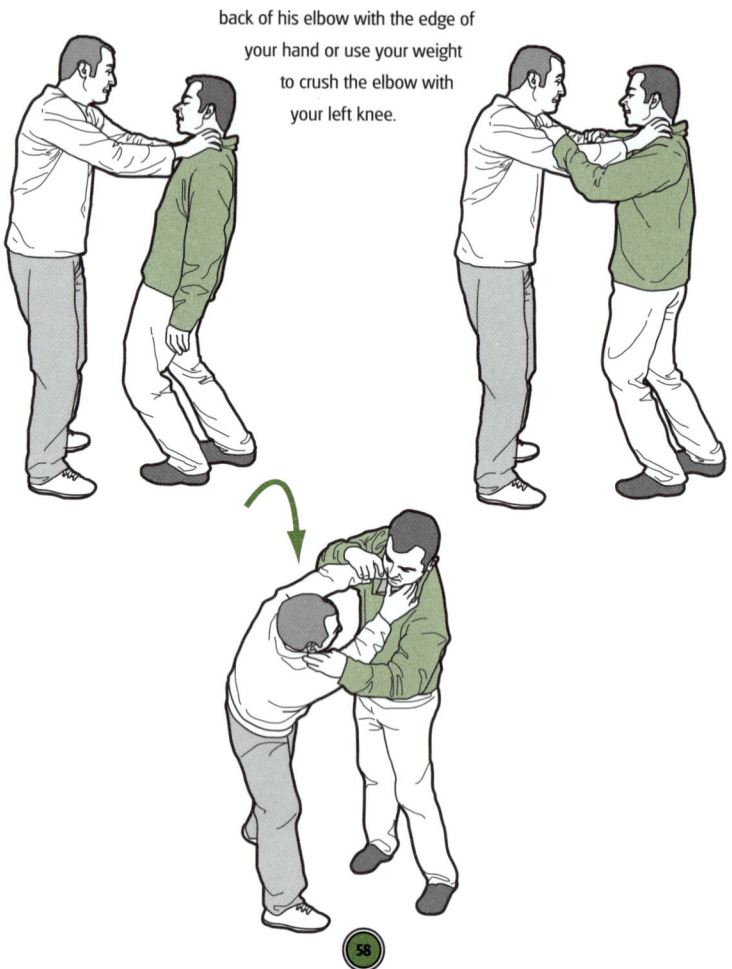

The Basics

ESCAPING THE REAR HAIR HOLD

If your hair is grabbed, lift your hands over your head and tightly grip the aggressor's wrist. As you do so, drop your body slightly and twist to your right quickly. As the grip breaks, keep your wrist hold and twist the arm, forcing the aggressor to bow down. Drop the weight of your body on to your left leg and deliver a powerful kick to his face, aiming for the nose.

The Basics

STRANGLEHOLDS

Approach the aggressor from behind or turn him around so that he is facing away from you. Throw your left arm around his throat so that your inner arm bone is in contact with and flattening his windpipe. Lift your right arm so you can grip its biceps with your left hand. Push your right hand behind the aggressor's head to force it forward, increasing constriction; unconsciousness soon follows. Drop to your knees quickly, still exerting pressure, to snap the aggressor's neck and kill him outright.

BACK-BREAK THROW

From the front, bend your legs so you can pass your right arm over the aggressor's chest while bringing your left hand behind his knees and forcing them forward to collapse him. Straighten and stand up, holding the aggressor at your chest height. Without stopping, step forward so that your right leg is below his body, and then drop down using his weight to smash him over your knee, breaking his back in the process. This technique may seem difficult, but is quite easy to master; practicing the lift stage will give you confidence.

Choose your weapon

Ideally, use a knife designed for killing. Drawing a knife escalates any confrontation to lethal violence. Keep a very good hold on it so that it cannot be used against you.

The Basics

Aiming the chair in a diamond shape ensures that the aggressor is hit with at least two legs; squared legs may go to either side of his body and miss him.

SURVIVING A KNIFE ATTACK

Knives are popular because they are easy to obtain and hide. If attacked with a knife, you can be sure the aggressor is out to inflict as much damage as he possibly can. A chair, held close to your chest, will defend you against the initial attack. When possible, hold the chair out and run at the aggressor, aiming the legs at his face and upper chest.

THE KILLER BLOW

In many cases, you will only have one chance to overpower an aggressor. You need a blow that will do the most damage, even if you are not strong or used to fighting. Hold the end of a tightly-rolled newspaper or a matchbox in your fist so that the item protrudes a little from the thumb side of the fist. This deals a devastating blow that smashes facial bones. Use a wide, strong swing and aim to hit anywhere between the cheekbone and lower jaw. This blow will snap the lower jaw if it hits it squarely, maybe even killing the aggressor.

THE EAR-SLAP

The inner ears are used for both hearing and balance. If your hands are free and the aggressor is in striking distance (or holding you), cup your hands, fingers tightly closed to make a seal, and clap them as fast and hard as possible to both ears simultaneously. This compresses air in the inner ears, bursting the eardrums and wrecking balance, co-ordination and hearing. Even one hand clapping can be devastating.

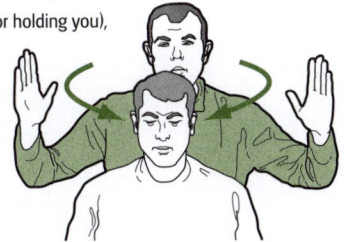

The Basics

DISARMING A GUNMAN

A gun ready and aimed at you may seem impossible to survive, but with speed of thought and action you may still win. You are still alive; the aggressor is waiting for some reason, and that is in your favour. Assume he will shoot you sooner or later, even if hesitant. He has pulled a gun on you, and must be desperate. If he tells you to move, do so. If he can see that you are scared and carrying out his instructions without hesitation, he may relax and get close enough to allow you to disarm him.

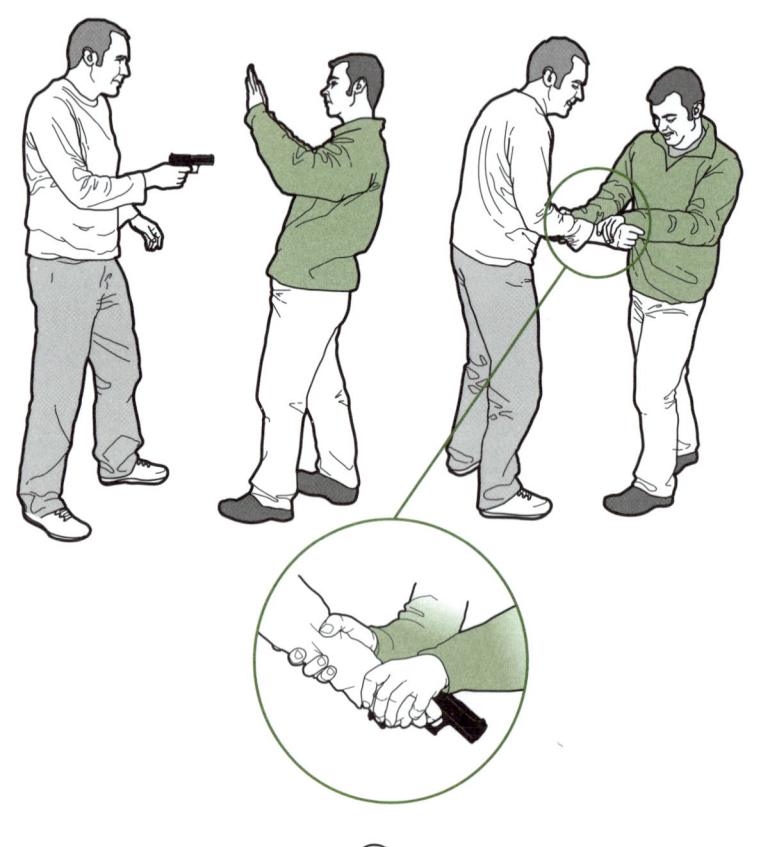

The Basics

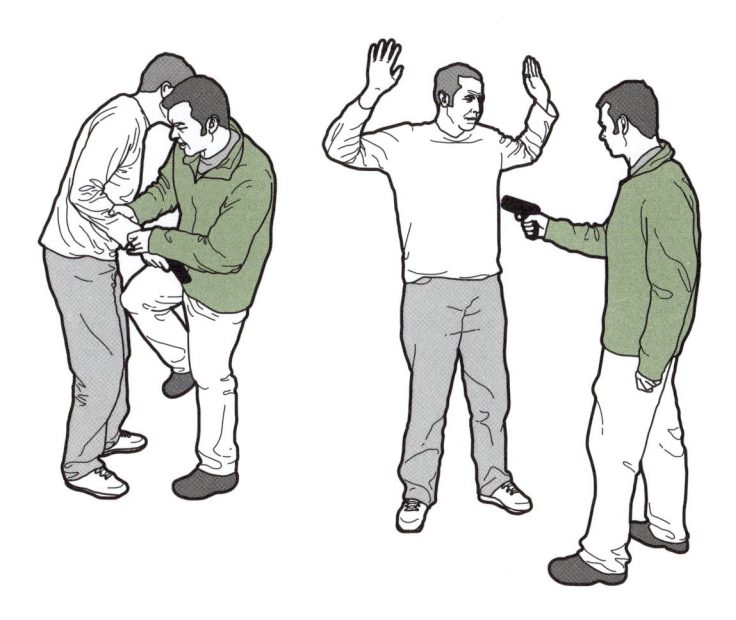

Short-barrelled guns are designed for killing in confined spaces.
Wait until the aggressor is close to you before disarming him.
Once you have the gun, fire immediately.

As soon as opportunity arises, quickly hit, grab and gouge his wrist, turning slightly to your side so that if he shoots, there is less of a target to hit. Use your free hand to grasp the gun and turn it away from you. Twist the aggressor's hand to force him to release his grip. Further distract him simultaneously by kneeing his groin and head-butting him as he bends forward. As soon as you have the gun, aim and fire it. Do not hesitate, even if he pretends to surrender. You would not have been able to disarm him if he had just shot you immediately. Do not risk him disarming you!

⚠ Acts of Terror

Nowadays terrorists may strike almost anywhere, and there is a chance you might be subjected to some form of terrorist attack. The events of September 11, 2001 – terrible though they undoubtedly were – formed a highly successful terrorist plan. It woke the world up to the power of terrorism and the terrorists' total disregard for innocent people.

HIJACKING

Taking control of a vehicle to use as a weapon of destruction is not, strictly speaking, hijacking. Hijacking assumes that the terrorists have demands, and have chosen a passenger vehicle to use hostages as a tool of negotiation to either attain those demands or to gain publicity for them. In a 9/11-style attack, you can do no better than the brave passengers of United Airlines Flight 93, and try your best to overpower your attackers. There is literally nothing to lose.

World governments never give in to hijackers' demands, and desired results are rarely attained. This leaves hijacked passengers and crews to undergo long periods of high stress – often resulting in eventual release, but occasionally in death.

This is a very tough survival challenge, but the basics are the same, and you will benefit from knowledge, confidence, physical and psychological condition, a sense of humour and the will to survive. The usual priorities of protection, location, water and food still apply. Your best personal approach is to adopt as low a profile as possible.

BLENDING IN

When hijacked, it is vital to assess the hijackers right away, and ascertain their political and religious beliefs, their aims, even the actual group they belong to. Generally, you will be told these things early on. If your politics, beliefs or nationality do not conflict with the hijackers', your chances of surviving are slightly higher than those of someone to whom this does not apply. If someone is executed to prove a point, the hijackers are more likely to pick someone they dislike. If you are unlucky enough to simply be from the wrong place, avoid attracting attention and hope someone less astute gets noticed. Terrorists often choose victims who make themselves known. Avoid being singled out at all costs.

You can expect to be kept for some time with your hands on your head. Sitting in this position for long periods causes severe pain. Bindings are unpleasant, and also cause severe pain and discomfort. Your only respite is flexing your muscles and expanding your limbs when you get the chance. Never complain or move position, as this will only single you out. Suffer in silence and let other, less knowledgeable detainees take up the issues if they choose to. They may find a sympathetic ear, or begin the selection process of the first victim (or both), but either way you benefit.

IN EXTREMIS

Despite all your efforts, hijackers may become violent towards you. At this stage, there is very little you can do. If you are absolutely sure you can overpower the terrorists – or you are certain they are about to take your life – then fight. Otherwise, resistance will only make the situation worse, so do your best to take it. Show pain naturally, when it hurts. Showing pain too early can make the aggressor impatient and more violent; trying to show how 'tough' you are will just get you beaten to death.

Gaining the respect of your captors through arrogant resistance only happens in movies. If you decide to risk playing games, try to build a relationship; if you can get a good rapport, it often leads to survival. If not, of course, you'll be the first victim.

Your bearing will affect the way you are treated. Some people have a 'military style' about them; they walk upright, with an air of authority. Avoid this at all costs, as the terrorists, who will be used to the police and military, will assume you are a soldier or undercover operator and eliminate you. On the other hand, slouching and looking unconcerned will mark you out as an arrogant troublemaker. Being aware of your body language and adjusting it accordingly is a very important skill.

COMMUNICATING WITH TERRORISTS

Communication, or the lack of it, is a difficult area. Your non-verbal communication will begin the process. It is hard to get the balance right; showing hate is as provocative as showing compassion in some situations. Try to look attentive, obedient and meek. Inevitably, any communication will single you out and defeat the object of keeping a low profile.

Avoid deep eye-to-eye contact, but do not avoid eye contact altogether, as this is antagonistic. Blatantly looking away from your aggressor is as much an act of defiance as staring.

Acts of Terror

You will probably be unaware of your destination and of the terrorists' demands. What will be apparent to you is the time you have spent on the ground. Experienced hijackers will insist on hops from airport to airport en route to the destination; these reduce the risk of armed military assault. Before risking armed rescue, the authorities must try all the options, attempt to negotiate a settlement and fully explore the legal and political implications of an armed assault. This all takes time. The decision may involve people from different countries and with opposite views; just getting them together may take three days.

RESCUE ATTEMPTS

The decision to use military force is only ever made after all other efforts have failed, when the lives of the hostages are seriously at risk. The country you are in may also not have a properly trained anti-terrorist force. Specialists may have to be brought in to oversee the crisis or effect an armed response. Information gathered by the authorities needs to be correlated and assessed, and again this takes time.

Even an experienced anti-terrorist team has its limitations. The aircraft may have been flown through restricted airspace, and the observers' surveillance craft not allowed to follow. If the plane is flying from place to place, then the team may monitor its fuel consumption and plan an assault when the plane has to refuel at the next stop. Available refuelling facilities can be identified and assaults planned at likely locations. Airports may try to manage the situation so that the plane has to land at a facility that has been pre-selected as the best rescue venue; in these situations, the actual assault can be launched relatively quickly.

RELEASE

As a goodwill gesture, hijackers often release some hostages. If you are so lucky, the authorities will need to interview you as soon as possible to get a better idea of the threat. While still a hostage, make mental notes of events and descriptions of the terrorists, their ages, the weapons they have, where they usually stand and any specific idiosyncrasies. This information will be of great importance to the negotiators and other officials. If you are not released early, your chances of being involved in some form of armed conflict will have increased. The situation may resolve peacefully, but you must remain alert to the possibility of an assault and prepare yourself to react positively. Most assaults begin with stun grenades; these cause a shock wave that affects your hearing, balance and co-ordination for a time. Never try to run; you will be badly unbalanced, and you are liable to run straight

Acts of Terror

into a hail of bullets. The best bet is to drop to the floor and curl small, hands out flat so people can see you are unarmed. If possible, stay like this until you are ordered to move – hopefully by a friendly force. If you have to move because of fire or other hazard, stay low and, if possible, evacuate the aircraft. Once outside, stay down and get clear of the aircraft if you can. If you are not sure where to go, lie down and stay in position until you are told to move.

SURVIVOR'S GUILT

If you survive a hijacking, you may have stood by while others were executed, even possibly because you kept a low profile. This can bring intense – but inappropriate – guilt. You have survived an encounter with people who have no scruples about killing, and you are not responsible for the actions of others.

KIDNAPPING

Kidnapping someone and taking them hostage is a common terrorist act. Much of the advice on hijacking applies to hostage situations, although obviously it is impossible to keep a low profile when you are the only one involved. The fact that you are being taken alive suggests that the kidnappers have some use for you – to start with, anyway. This is the key to your early survival: they will hesitate before killing you, and will be reluctant to risk the noise of shooting at you in a normal district. From the first moment, you should be seeking to escape; the longer you are held, the harder escape gets. When first captured, you will probably be somewhere comparatively normal, so if you can escape, chances are you can find help locally. However, once out of the area, you will not know where you are or whom you can trust if you do escape.

BEING TIED

As soon as you are kidnapped, you will probably be tied and gagged. Even so, there is a chance of a quick escape, as the kidnappers will be rushed. You must present parts of your body for binding so that the ties can be loosened afterwards.

Offer your hands in front of your body, keeping the heels of your hands together and slightly cupping them. At the same time, keep your hands close to your body with your elbows pushed out, which causes your wrists to part. Binding you like this lets you straighten your arms later, which pushes your wrists together and loosens the bindings. Flattening your hands palm to palm will further loosen them until you can wriggle free.

If a gag is used, push your chin on your chest and puff your cheeks out; if at all possible, also keep your teeth tightly closed. This again lets you loosen your bindings when you draw your chin up, open your teeth and stretch your neck to its full extent. If your hands are being tied behind your back, present them thumb to thumb with palms outwards and arms slightly bent. Try to ensure that there is a good gap between your wrists. Turning your hands palm to palm and drawing them up your back will loosen the binding.

Having loosened your bindings, you may be able to surprise your captors by escaping when they are distracted. Running from a building into a street full of local people will bring immediate attention to you, and kidnappers are unlikely to risk retaking you in full view.

ESCAPING CARS

If you do not escape kidnapping immediately, you will probably be moved in the back of a vehicle. If you are gagged, you may be made to lie in the rear seat well and covered over. If you are not gagged, you might be sat in the back with a guard. In either case, consider escaping by loosening your bindings and quickly opening the door and jumping out as the vehicle starts moving (do not do this at speed). In a city or town, the vehicle will often have to slow down or stop. An ideal jump time is when the vehicle is pulling away from traffic lights – force the door open and throw yourself out of the near side, avoiding passing vehicles. Cuts and bruises are nothing compared to being a hostage. Once out of built-up areas, you will be travelling at speed and passing through quiet areas, and the chances then are that you will have to wait a long time for another opportunity.

SURVIVING CAPTIVITY

Once you have been kidnapped, your priority has to be surviving until an escape opportunity presents itself, or you are released. In early stages, hostages are often very confused and exceptionally vulnerable. They mistrust their captors, and in group situations there is also mistrust of oneself and others. Keeping the mind positively active is vital; dwelling on negative thoughts destroys the will to survive. Never let the mind relax, but keep it running. This is best accomplished by having a personal project, such as constructing an imaginary luxury home. This doesn't mean just thinking about the building; it means planning every minor detail, the materials needed, the human resources, the actual building of it, brick by brick. The one thing your captors cannot take from you is your

Acts of Terror

inner self. You must keep this part totally in your control at all times. Being in isolation, with minimum human contact, leads to hopelessness you must overcome. The only emotional support for you is you! Living without affection of any kind can eat away at you, and you must guard against this. Political hostages are often forced to make undesirable public statements. Your not wanting to make such statements is almost expected, so isolation, tiredness and uncertainty are used to wear you down until you will say anything. Your captors will try everything to domineer, but they have to break you. A common way is to threaten to take your life. Having the courage to accept that you may die takes away the most powerful lever your enemies have. It can become a battle of wills. In these situations, the captor loses if he takes the hostage's life, so he tries to keep the hostage alive from fear of failure.

THE DROP TECHNIQUE TO ESCAPE BUILDINGS

Hostages are usually held in a building, often not far from a busy street and people who can help. Have no doubt; escape is often in your best interests. You may be held in decent surroundings and treated well – perhaps because negotiations are going on to secure your release. There certainly will be action being taken to help you by outside agencies. However,

Having decided that your survival depends on escaping, the last thing you want is to sustain an injury on your way out

only you can decide whether or not your life is at risk and whether escape is a possibility.

If your survival depends on escaping, you should plan a prepared escape if at all possible. If not, you will have to hope for a chance opportunity. Your escape route will probably include a drop, and proper landing lessens the risk of recapture from injury. With higher drops, look for the softest place to land; if you can, try to cushion your fall with clothing, bedding or other soft material. A careful three-storey drop is eminently survivable; a seven-storey drop usually fatal.

Ease yourself over the edge of the drop, facing the building. Keep one hand holding on until your arm is fully stretched; look down for the safest spot to land. While still holding on, place your free hand on the wall and push yourself away as you let go. This keeps you clear of the building during your descent, and should spin you to face away. Keep looking at the landing spot. Keep your ankles and knees pressed together, with your legs slightly bent at the knees. Push your chin on to your chest and keep your teeth clenched. Pull your hands up to the sides of your head, and land on the balls of the feet, not your heels.

As you hit, force your knees to the side. This, combined with the forward force of your body, will turn you so that you roll on to the ground, spreading the impact and greatly reducing the chance of injury. Once you are safely on the ground, make good your escape.

Tips To Avoid Kidnapping

- Be aware when you could be a target, and avoid drawing attention
- If you are in a foreign country, dress down and avoid any conflict or debate, especially political or religious
- Do not drive alone, especially in hire cars or cars with foreign plates
- Only use approved taxicabs
- On foot, face oncoming traffic to lessen the risk of them approaching by car from behind
- Change your routines regularly to make planning your kidnapping difficult

TERRORIST BOMBINGS

The way terrorists plant bombs differs from organization to organization. Bombs can be in cars or vans, in bins, in luggage, on people; detonated by timer or radio or hand, with or without warning. If you suspect – or are told – that there is a bomb in the area, leave immediately.

Acts of Terror

If you are not sure where it is, the safest stance is to leave any building and lie face-down outside. If you can quickly get a good distance from buildings and into a large open space, do so. If not, lie against an outside wall well away from items – such as bins, post boxes and motorbikes – that can turn into shrapnel. Tuck yourself tight in to the wall. Cover your ears, and keep your face on the ground, turned slightly towards the building.

If you are near the bomb when it blows, you will feel heat, and notice oxygen being pulled from your lungs. Shockwaves spread quickly, destroying most things in their path, but lessen in power as they radiate away. Close to the ground, the waves should be less violent; the building will absorb some of the shock, and bounce other waves away from you. Having survived the initial blast, stay where you are until you absolutely certain there is no chance of a second explosion.

If the buildings start collapsing, stay where you are. Generally, buildings fall away from the foundations, leaving a comparatively safe zone of a metre or so between building and debris. Rescue teams will soon be searching through the wreckage.

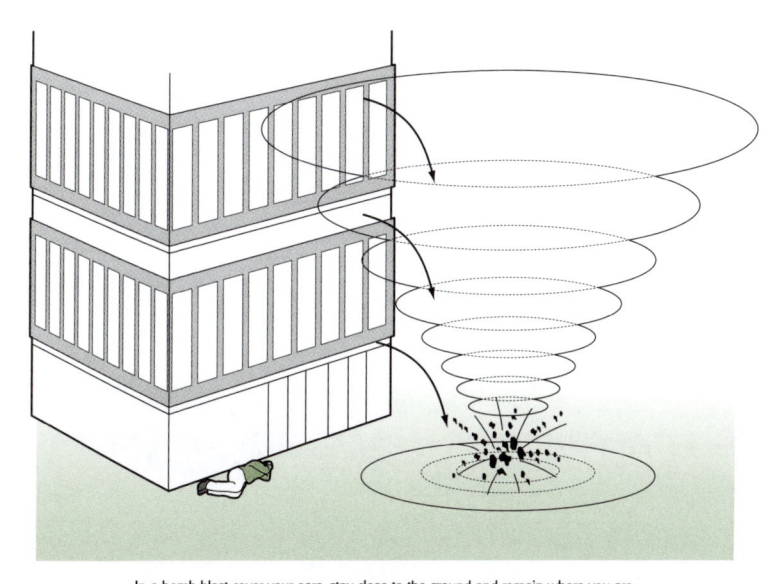

In a bomb blast cover your ears, stay close to the ground and remain where you are.

LETTER AND PARCEL BOMBS

Terrorist packages are designed to kill or incapacitate when opened. If for any reason you are suspicious, respect that and immediately act to safeguard yourself and those around you. If your instinct is wrong, there is no harm done, and much potential disaster averted.

Suspect packages and letters may be delivered by hand, placed through the letterbox or left nearby. If this is unusual, your suspicion should be heightened. Posted devices are often sent from another country. Checking stamps and postmarks of unsolicited mail can alert you to potential danger. There may be far more stamps used than necessary. The delivery name and address may also be slightly incorrect, or hand-written in a clearly foreign hand. Poor spelling and writing are also common.

Devices may be wrapped with a large amount of tape, be grease-stained and/or smell of marzipan or almonds. Packages are also often much heavier than you would expect, while both letters and packages may have uneven weight distribution.

Once you suspect a device, leave the area immediately, taking other people with you. If indoors, open all windows and doors. Do not switch any electrical equipment or lights on or off, or activate any fire alarms. Never examine suspect devices – leave it to experts.

Know the score

Practice and experience will give you confidence in an emergency.

Surviving Terrorism

In response to escalating terrorist acts government, military, police and security personnel around the world work together by sharing information and intelligence that allows them to analyze the current threat they are faced with, as well as respond to emerging trends. This intelligence is then used to develop the most effective way of dealing with the threat and the best techniques for the general public to employ to give them the chance of surviving a terrorist incident.

Quite simply, you are a target – we all are – and so we all need to be vigilant and expect and react effectively to whatever danger we are subjected to. Terrorists, by the very nature of the business they are in, are looking for opportunities to further their cause by gaining as much publicity as possible so the bigger the terror they inflict, the more likely the media exposure they get, be it from a single person carrying out an attack (commonly known as a "lone wolf") to a highly sophisticated, meticulously planned attack by well-trained insurgents. This need to gain publicity is often the Achilles heel. There's little use in carrying out a terrorist attack in a remote field, miles away from anyone, with no media coverage. What would be the point? The result is that the majority of attacks are in highly populated areas or locations that have some religious, military or political significance. Consequently, it is within these areas that we must be particularly alert. That's not to say that you should switch off in other locations. An attack can happen anywhere, at any time by the most innocuous-looking person. Rarely do terrorists plan, train and equip themselves in the location of the proposed attack. They may visit the selected site for reconnaissance purposes but are unlikely to draw too much attention to themselves. However, pre-planning activity away from the area of attack is where they may let their guard down enough to raise suspicion.

Becoming suspicious of people or situations is an innate survival instinct present in us all. On many occasions, I have experienced what can only be described as feelings of unease, which quickly put me on my guard. In every case, it was the precursor to a dangerous event. Always trust and act on your "gut" feeling. Above all, you must stay safe.

Before it happens, plan for the possibility. Think about what action you are going to take if faced with an incident. What plans are already in place in your location? Is there an emergency evacuation procedure? If so, have you checked it out, walked the route, located the safe area?

The accepted procedure adopted and taught by the UK authorities is Run, Hide and Tell.

RUN

From the moment you suspect a dangerous situation, or on hearing what you consider to be gunshots or an explosion, don't look for the cause. Immediately make good your escape by moving in the opposite direction as quickly as possible, making sure you keep your wits about you just in case there is another incident occurring along your route. If you have had time to plan a safe route, stick to it unless it exposes you to further danger. Remember, people around you may not have your knowledge so take control and insist they leave with you. If they don't, you must keep to your plan. Do not carry bags, etc. as they will impede safe progress.

HIDE

If there's no option to remove yourself, your next option is to hide. Immediately put your phone on "Silent" and turn off the "Vibrate" option. If you can't do this, switch it off altogether. Likewise, if it's dark, turn it off if you can't stop the illumination mode. It's a real giveaway in a dimly lit hiding place, powerful enough to show through your clothing, especially pockets. It helps if you have already decided on a good place to hide. If not, you are left with snap decisions. Either way, make sure you are in a place of safety that has substantial brick or concrete walls and secure exits; try not to get trapped in a room with no exit other than the way you came in.

Guns are powerful weapons and even small-arms fire can penetrate brick, wood and metal. Standing behind doors will not be sufficient cover so move away, keeping low to the floor at all times. Lock the doors and, where possible, wedge them too. (Keep ready-made wedges in your luggage when travelling, routinely using them to further secure your hotel room doors.) If you have time, pile heavy furniture, office cabinets, etc. behind the doors, continually building a secure barrier, but do not expose yourself in the process.

Having experienced a terrorist shooter, I can verify that walls and doors are no obstacle to high-velocity bullets. In my encounter, bullets came through a door frame, two walls, a filing cabinet and embedded themselves two thirds of the way through a third brick wall at waist height. Thankfully, I was lying down at the time!

Acting dead is not a good survival option. It may work, but many terrorists routinely shoot at the bodies of their victims.

TELL

Part of your terrorist survival procedures should be to know exactly how to summon help in whatever environment you find yourself in. Always make sure that you have a serviceable mobile device and that you have keyed in the local law enforcement numbers to summon help or to report an incident or possible hazard. Make sure that you are not having to dial numbers at the time of crisis; you should be ready to just press "Send" to save time and alleviate possible mistaken dialling and panicked delay.

Don't hang around recording the events. If you can see the attacker, they can see you! Standing around taking a photograph or video is not a good survival technique. Once you are in a safe place, immediately contact the authorities, giving them as much information as possible, with emphasis on how many terrorists you have seen, where they are or where the incident is taking place. If you can describe the perpetrators, all the better.

It helps if you have developed your recognition and recall skills in advance. A good way of doing this is to practise the skill of quickly taking the main features of people you meet in everyday life and recalling your description of them later to see how much you have retained and how accurate your recall was. Using "lookalike" tagging by taking the overall appearance and assigning this to known individuals – for example, using famous people as the prompt: "the guy looked like Donald Trump", etc. – is a good way of conveying the description. It will help the authorities if you can further recall a description of the clothing, weapons, equipment and the number of attackers involved. If you have managed to get away from the danger, make sure you have left your contact details with a member of the security forces or contact them as soon after the incident as possible. You could have valuable information.

If you have not been able to clear the area, you may be faced with a range of armed response units: some in uniform, some not. This is a dangerous time as the armed personnel will probably not be in a position to positively identify the attackers and, as such, everyone they come into contact with will be treated as a possible threat. They will also be high on adrenalin themselves and, no matter how much training they have, they will be making snap decisions under extreme personal pressure. If confronted, do not run toward them unless told to do so, do not shout and wave your arms about, do not make any sudden moves or move towards your clothing or pockets as this may be perceived as an attempt to draw a weapon or activate an explosive device. It will help if you can keep calm and help those around you to do exactly what the armed response officers tell them.

If you have been unfortunate enough to have driven into a dangerous situation such as a riot, or active terrorist attack, you will have to act quickly to make your decision to stay with your vehicle or leave it. Remember, a car or van, etc. offers no real protection from bullets or explosives.

The chance of you being able to carry out an emergency "handbrake turn" without training is unlikely. The chance of you losing control and ploughing into a crowd or into the line of terrorist fire is a real possibility though. Reversing out could be your best option, depending on the traffic. Before you are faced with this possibility, take the opportunity to practise fast reverse driving. It is not as simple as you may think: under pressure, drivers may struggle to engage reverse and can easily stall the vehicle, rendering themselves and any other occupants helpless. Before you have to do so in an emergency, practise getting in and out of your vehicle in a hurry. You will be surprised how long it takes and how difficult it is to get from the driving seat out through the passenger door. Again, before it happens for real, train your family to know what to do and how to get out of the vehicle quickly and safely. This doesn't have to be as a result of a terrorist attack, it could simply be that the car has burst into flames on a busy motorway. Think about it: practising with the kids might seem extreme, but if it prevents them from panicking and exiting in the line of motorway traffic, it's worth it!

If you are familiar with the area, obviously your chances of fleeing using the vehicle will be better. If you are a visitor, you may not know that the next turn leads to a blind alley! If faced with a situation like this, it is probably better to vacate the vehicle, leaving it and any belongings behind. Fumbling around gathering your belongings will further expose you to the danger you are trying to escape from. Once on foot, follow the Run, Hide, Tell, advice described earlier.

VEHICLE ATTACK

Where possible, always walk facing oncoming traffic. This gives you the opportunity to see if a vehicle is veering towards you, giving you the split second you may need to avoid a collision.

Surviving Terrorism

In any event, when walking, stay vigilant. Make sure you take note of possible escape routes – for example, an alleyway, building entrance, etc. Keep as far away from the road edge as you can. Walk close to buildings, or between the street furniture – i.e. substantial lamp posts, iron railings, bollards, signage, etc. – using these as barriers to a marauding vehicle. Choose your route with this in mind. It's better to cross the road to walk along a tree-lined, kiosk-filled boulevard than stay on the side with little or no obstruction to hamper an attack.

If you are involved in this type of attack, assume that if the vehicle comes to a halt, there will probably be a follow-up weapon attack. This may include explosives, possibly planted in the vehicle, waiting to be detonated. Assume this and move away or take adequate cover as quickly as possible, even if the terrorists have left the area, been restrained, injured or killed. You should also assume that there could be other terrorists in the vicinity not openly involved in the main incident but ready to attack when the time is right. Be extra vigilant post attack, don't assume you are safe when the authorities arrive. A follow-up attack is likely to be carried out when the authorities are exposed and vulnerable.

As time goes on, terrorists will develop other ways of perpetrating acts of terror. Good survival training includes keeping up to date with developing modus operandi and adapting to this by thinking through possible outcomes and practising your responses.

⚠ New and Cyber Threats to Survival

"Cyberspace is the term used to describe the electronic medium of digital networks used to store, modify and communicate information. It includes the Internet but also other information systems that support businesses, infrastructure and services."

Source: Security Service, MI5

Today's communication, and consequently certain aspects of survival, are highly dependent on systems that are reliant on cyberspace. As a result, terrorists, rogue states, organized crime syndicates and others who would do us harm are constantly developing their use of this medium and using cybercrime to attack, threaten and organize illicit finances. All of these activities are directly associated with modern survival and personal protection. Not least when the systems fail.

Society has become more and more dependent on technology, which has in turn left us more and more vulnerable to new and unforeseen survival scenarios. For example, do you have a paper map in your car or hiking rucksack (and do you know how to use it?) or do you rely on a Satellite Navigation Global Positioning System (Satnav)? What if all electronic systems in your location failed, or were destroyed by an attack at the same time? Virtually everything, from your wristwatch to your car, mobile phone, national electricity, gas and water systems, is controlled by electronic components such as semiconductors and microprocessors and without them, modern society would come to a screeching halt.

Imagine no mobile phones, no Internet, no mains electricity, water or gas!

One possible threat to our infrastructure could be from a so-called "Cyber Attack", either from a rogue nation, terrorist organization, organized crime syndicate or even a teenager working from their bedroom. One example of this was the "WannaCry virus", which almost shut down the British National Health Service in 2017 and affected more than 200,000 computers in approximately 180 countries.

Great care should be exercised to keep all computer programs up to date and with anti-virus software installed. Many viruses are sent as attachments to emails so the message here is that if you don't know who it is from, DO NOT OPEN IT! If you have opened something in error that you are suspicious of, switch off your computer immediately using the power

New and Cyber Threats to Survival

switch and not the usual shut-down procedure. This may stop the virus being written into the main memory of the computer.

One spate of attacks was initiated by criminals loading a virus onto a memory stick emblazoned with the target organization's logo. This memory stick was then dropped onto the car park of the target organization. Some well-meaning employee picked up the memory stick, took it into the office and plugged it into a computer and the virus activated. You can guess the rest!

Another threat is the so-called Electromagnetic Pulse. Early in the days of atomic weapons the Americans detonated an atomic bomb which caused street lighting in Hawaii (over 1,000 miles away) to fail. In those days, before transistors came onto the scene, most electronic devices, such as wireless sets, relied on thermionic valves or tubes which are virtually immune to the effects I will describe below.

It was later found that the weapon emitted what is now known as an Electromagnetic Pulse (now shortened to EMP), which is a massive pulse of electromagnetic energy – effectively radio waves. This energy soaks into virtually any metal object (that effectively becomes an antenna), such as a mains electricity cable, overhead power cable, internal metalwork in a mobile phone or car body, which will quite literally fry any sensitive electronic components and devices connected to it.

Electromagnetic pulses may be generated naturally by the sun when coronal mass ejections – a type of solar activity – occur or ,most probably in this day and age, by nuclear weapons detonated high in the atmosphere. It has been estimated that a nuclear device detonated over the Continental USA at an altitude of 300 miles or so would bring the whole country to a halt, causing massive damage to critical infrastructure and the resultant loss of life.

It is believed that any nations or organizations that possess nuclear weapons could launch an EMP attack.

Military equipment is, on the whole, protected or, in the jargon, "Hardened" against EMP, and motor vehicles built before, say, 1980, should be relatively immune as they contain very few sensitive electronic components, such as engine management systems, which are very sensitive to EMP. (In fact, some US police departments have a device which shoots out a wire that sticks to the back of a fleeing vehicle and fires a high voltage along that wire, which disables the vehicle.)

At times of heightened tensions, some protection may be afforded to electronic devices by at least unplugging them from power sources, telephone lines and Internet cables. Better protection may be afforded by placing your devices inside what is known as a Faraday cage or screen (named after the British scientist, Michael Faraday). Sounds complicated, but this can simply be a sealed metal enclosure such as a metal biscuit tin or tobacco tin with the seals cleaned with wire wool or similar. The effect of this is to distribute the EMP energy over the outside surface of the container rather than allowing it to enter the electronic device inside. Larger objects could be placed in a closed, unplugged domestic microwave oven.

> "It should also be remembered that common survival items such as LED torches, solar panels and generators have electronic controllers inside them so will also need protection."
>
> Mark Elliott,
> former law enforcement officer and close protection trainer

Clearly, the above demonstrates the need to put into place a plan of action that will take account of the possible effects of an attack. It doesn't, however, take a catastrophic event to threaten our cyber existence or put us in the way of harm.

Personal information is a vital part of our personal and family safety. The communication of information and intelligence about us is something that we should take great care to guard at all times. Sharing any information can lead to our being compromised. The adherence to sharing life events and personal information on social media can, and does, lead to threats and an open door to our finances. I am amazed how foolish people are when using the many social media platforms available to them. Even those with sensitive employments share day-to-day events. Serving military personnel, law enforcement operatives and politicians give away vital information that could be used to inform a stalker, attacker, terrorist or enemy regime where they are, what they are doing and what they are going to be doing on an hourly basis. Sharing personal information is bad enough but many users include family members, friends and colleagues' information too. Organized criminals merely have to monitor this "traffic" to plan an abduction of a target or members of the target's family. Terrorists can, likewise, keep watch on possible targets or organizations. Enemy intelligence agencies may use the cached information available to them to learn about a prisoner of war they are questioning and can use family information as a lever to break a cover story.

Sadly, children and other vulnerable people are targeted by villains, sex offenders and fraudsters every minute of every day. Online bullying, often involving gangs of perpetrators,

New and Cyber Threats to Survival

Electronic communication devices need to be shielded from the effects of EMP. Adapting everyday items to good effect is a cost-effective survival skill.

makes life unbearable for the recipient to the point where suicide can sometimes seem the best option. As a competent Internet user, you have a responsibility to ensure that your personal details and sensitive information are not openly shared. You must also take responsibility to ensure the safety of the vulnerable users around you by employing the very latest technical developments to control access and physically take every opportunity to see what they are doing and who they are interacting with.

Don't become complacent: even if you have taken the above steps, always assume that all of your cyber devices can be compromised, and regularly monitor the latest technology and scams being used by hackers, etc. There is plenty of software available to build a security barrier against hackers but don't assume that once it is employed, it will continue to be effective. The bad guys soon develop software to get around the good guys' security. Hackers are constantly looking for openings often presented to them by users who have not downloaded the latest updates, so be warned! Counter-intelligence measures that have been developed to nullify malicious code used to deploy a virus cannot work if it hasn't been downloaded!

FIREWALLS

Another measure that any user may take is to install a firewall.

> "A firewall is a network security system designed to prevent unauthorized access to or from a private network.
>
> Firewalls can be implemented as both hardware and software, or a combination of both. Network firewalls are frequently used to prevent unauthorized Internet users from accessing private networks connected to the Internet, especially intranets. All messages entering or leaving the intranet pass through the firewall, which examines each message and blocks those that do not meet the specified security criteria. The firewall's purpose is to stop unauthorized contact or entry onto the system. However, a firewall does not remove things that are already on the computer or network. Anti-virus software is needed as well to handle malicious code that may slip through the firewall undetected."
>
> Source: Vangie Beal, Webopedia

PHISHING

Even when you have put in place the best available protection for your device, you can unwittingly give secure information away. "Phishing" is the term used to explain the practice of sending what looks like legitimate emails constructed to dupe the recipient into supplying sensitive information, such as credit card and bank details. Often the purpose is to obtain the passwords used for a variety of applications and access to personal information, all of which can be used for illegal practices and to gain sensitive information. To combat this possibility, don't answer, and immediately delete, unsolicited emails – even when they look as though they have come from a government or other similar "professional" source. If in doubt, contact the sender or organization by telephone and question their validity. Do not use a telephone number given within the email as this may well be a set-up. Trawl the Internet to verify the contact details.

PASSWORD ATTACK

Another way to learn a password is to use software that is specially developed for this purpose. The process is simple: the software is deployed to bombard the password "gate" running through a dictionary of terms, names, words and a combination of words and numbers until the password is found. It's all done in a matter of seconds. Regularly changing your password reduces the chances of gaining access and makes it difficult to detect. Using combinations of numbers and upper and lower case letters also helps.

MAN-IN-THE-MIDDLE ATTACK

Years ago, in the days of "fax machines", I worked on an investigation where international criminals gained access to company fax machines and reprogrammed them to send a third secret copy of the texts to a remote receiver, thereby allowing the sensitive information to be used for fraudulent purposes. This, in effect, is a "man-in-the-middle" attack, and the practice carried over as the computer succeeded the fax. In fact, it made the whole process easier as it no longer needed a physical visit to reconfigure the machine. The "trojan" can be placed simply by including it in an email and, once opened, it secretly embeds itself in the computer. There are literally hundreds of rogue software products out there, and more are being developed every day. Your cyber survival and personal security will rely on you being able to keep up with growing trends and keeping abreast of the software developed to combat it.

DISASTER RECOVERY

Continually backing up your "clean" information is a must. If you are attacked and your cyber presence is compromised, you can quickly retrieve your information and carry on using another device, or from a pre-determined "safe" location. Whether for yourself or your business, you should from hereon plan your disaster recovery, both for cyber and physical continuance. As pointed out earlier, some attacks can completely destroy electronic equipment and the information therein. You can download your most sensitive and needed information onto a memory stick, which can be kept in a secure place within a radiation-proof container. Then there are purpose-built secure facilities offering the best storage possible, although these come at a high price.

▲ Navigation on Land

When navigating on land, your first concern is to orient your map correctly, which can be done in one of two ways: with a compass, or by visual means. Setting it visually involves turning it until the map features correspond with the position of the same features on the ground. This is simple and effective, but requires practice.

Get to a local position with a good view and open a local-area map the normal way up. The top is generally northerly. Find a prominent ground feature that is easily identifiable on your map, such as a railway bridge, lake, or church. Turn the map in front of you, until the symbols align with the ground features.

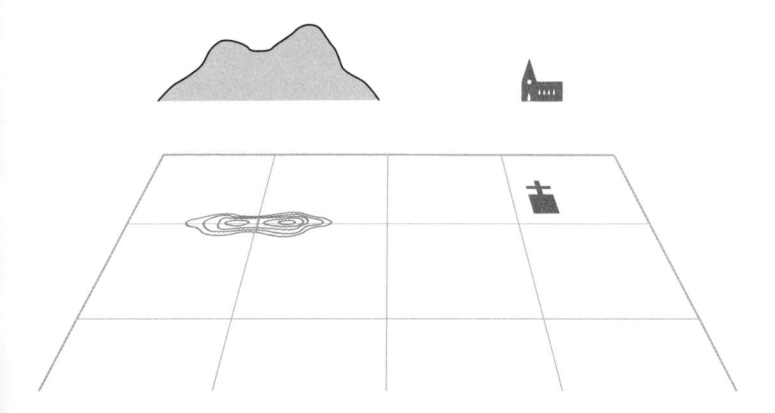

A common mistake is to stick to reading maps with the print the correct way up. In reality, the map can – and should – be read the way you are facing. Once you are confident using prominent features, practice on less identifiable ones, such as the contours of the land. Double-check via prominent features. It is very easy to mistake one hill for another – especially under pressure.

Navigation on Land

FINDING THE DIRECTION

Direction from your location to a destination is expressed in angular degrees, from 0° to 360°. There are 16 main directions.

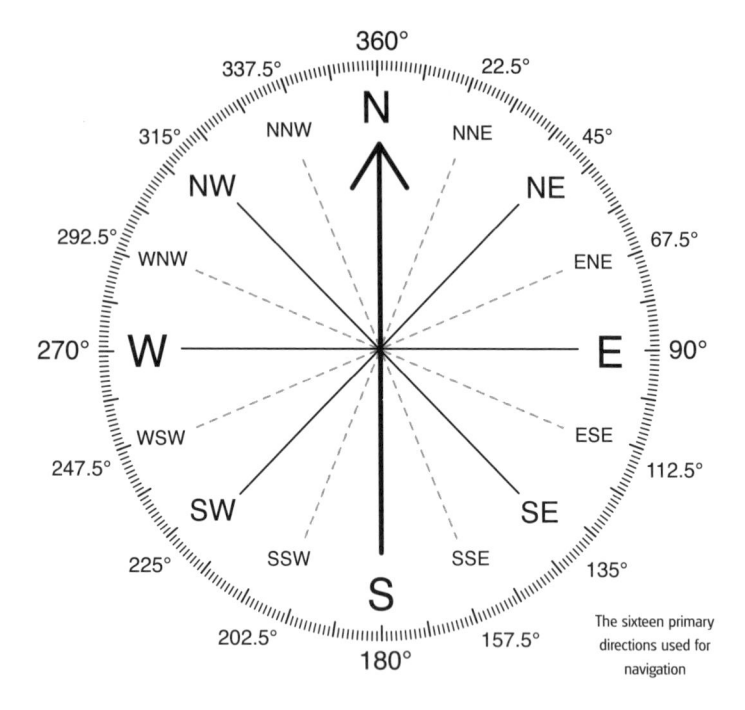

The sixteen primary directions used for navigation

Using a compass enhances your map-reading. Place the centre over your position on the map, lining up the north arrow with the north-south lines on your map's grid. You can then follow your destination's direction.

GIVING A SIX-FIGURE MAP REFERENCE

You may need to use map references to direct rescuers or to locate a safe area. In either case, a mistake may prove fatal. Maps are criss-crossed with a grid. These lines are numbered by two-figure numbers shown in the margin, running from east to west and south to north.

Navigation on Land

To reference a particular grid square, you need to know that the first two digits of a six-figure reference are the number of the easting (vertical) line that touches its bottom left corner, and the fourth and fifth digits are the number of the northing (horizontal) line that touches the same bottom left corner. With a number, trace the lines to their intersection to find the square; with a square, follow the lines to the margin to find the numbers.

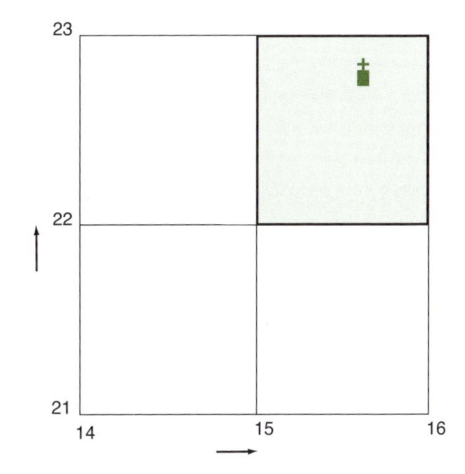

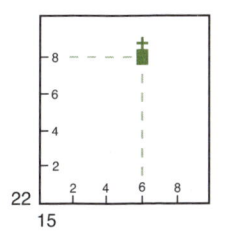

The church at 6,8 within square 15-22 is referenced as 156 228.

A specific location within the square is referenced by breaking down the square into tenths horizontally and vertically. The map should have a Romer scale that shows the tenths within a grid square. Imagine the grid square divided into tenths horizontally and vertically and visualise imaginary lines that intersect at the target. This will give you two single numbers. The easting horizontal number goes in third place, and the northing vertical number in sixth place.

Eastings before northings

The golden rule when giving map references is to give eastings before northings (ie. the horizontal number first). Remember this as 'E' and 'Horizontal' coming before 'N' and 'Vertical' in the alphabet.

Navigation on Land

USING GRID LETTERS

The British national mapping grid is divided into 100,000 lettered squares. This means the same numbers are duplicated on sheets in the same series. This can be disastrous if you send a rescue team to the wrong map sheet. To make map references absolutely clear, always give prefixed map-sheet letters before the six-digit number. You should also record the map's serial number in case verification is needed.

COMPASSES

In recent years, satellite navigation has largely replaced traditional navigation. Nevertheless, I strongly believe it remains important to learn basic navigation using a compass. A compass indicates direction from a fixed line (north-south). Simply, it is a magnetic needle, on a pivot over a card, which can swing freely until it rests pointing to magnetic north.

The Chinese were aware of the principle in the 1st century BC, but our first sensitive and accurate instrument was Kelvin's dry compass, invented in 1876. This excellent design is still used in merchant shipping today. In 1882, a water-filled compass was invented that allowed the needle to rest much more quickly, making readings faster. Today's lightweight compass uses the same principle, but is filled with oil.

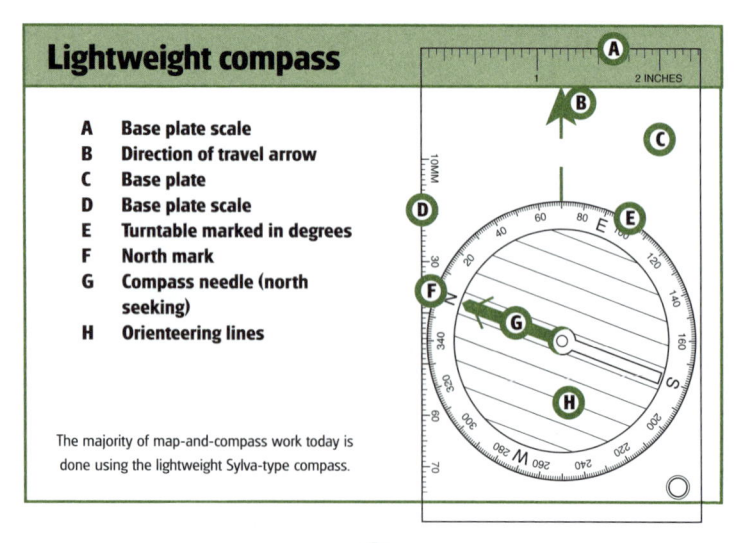

Lightweight compass

- **A** Base plate scale
- **B** Direction of travel arrow
- **C** Base plate
- **D** Base plate scale
- **E** Turntable marked in degrees
- **F** North mark
- **G** Compass needle (north seeking)
- **H** Orienteering lines

The majority of map-and-compass work today is done using the lightweight Sylva-type compass.

USING A COMPASS

A compass needle points to magnetic north, a spot approximately 1,400 miles (2.250km) south of the North Pole, off the Canadian coast. This means we have three norths in map-and-compass work:

- ▲ **True North** – the North Pole
- ▲ **Grid North** – the north shown by the map's grid system
- ▲ **Magnetic North** – the direction in which a magnetized needle points.

A compass lets you find direction and bearings from your position, follow a bearing accurately, walk in a straight line and return to your starting position.

FINDING DIRECTION USING BEARINGS

Practice makes perfect. Obtain a lightweight compass and go to an open location, such as your local park or playing fields. Choose a feature some distance away, and hold the compass above the waist in the palm of your hand, ensuring that it is level enough to allow the needle to swing freely. Point the direction-of-travel arrow at the feature you have chosen. Keeping the compass level and in position, swivel the turntable so that the orienteering arrow falls directly below the north side of the magnetic needle. Read off the bearing given at the base of the direction-of-travel arrow. This bearing is the magnetic bearing to your chosen feature.

WALKING A STRAIGHT LINE USING A COMPASS

Choose a bearing, and rotate your compass so that the chosen bearing is in line with the direction-of-travel arrow. Now turn yourself so that the north arrow of the magnetic needle moves over the orienteering arrow. Now simply follow the direction-of-travel arrow, making sure you keep the magnetic needle in position over the orienteering arrow. You can return to your starting position by simply adding 180° to your original bearing, and following that back.

COMPASS ERROR

Every compass has some degree of individual error and may read a few degrees away from magnetic north. Check regularly using a known bearing or against another compass of known error. Compass needles are magnetic, and can be attracted by iron, steel, overhead cables, buried pipelines and certain rocks. Even so, a compass is the most useful navigation aid. Mistrusting the compass and relying on your senses is a recipe for disaster.

Navigation on Land

MAP ERROR

Maps indicate magnetic north at time of printing. Unfortunately, magnetic north moves each year. Most maps list average annual change and their print year so you can compensate.

SETTING A MAP WITH A COMPASS

First, calculate the map error from the information it gives, and adjust your compass. For example, if the magnetic variation is 7° west of grid north, you would have to adjust the compass orienteering arrow by this figure. Then place the compass on the map so that the direction-of-travel arrow points north up an easting grid line. Turn the map and compass until the north of the magnetic needle falls over the orienteering arrow, making sure the orienteering arrow remains parallel to the grid lines.

FINDING YOUR EXACT POSITION

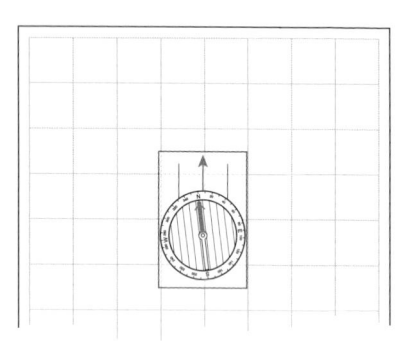

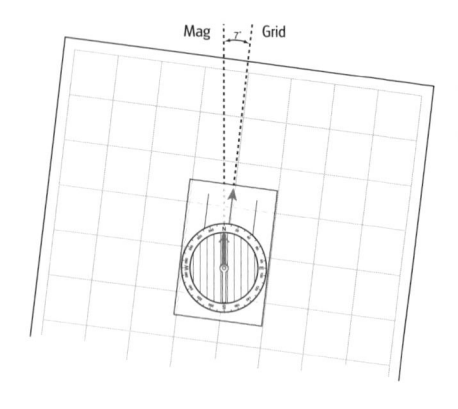

To find your exact position on a map, you need to select two ground features marked on your map, such as a hilltop and a church. Take a bearing, as explained earlier, by holding the compass level, pointing the direction-of-travel arrow at the feature, and adjusting the turntable so that the north side of the needle falls over the orienteering arrow. Remember to convert this to a grid bearing by subtracting the map variation. A magnetic bearing of 340° symbol with variation of 7° would mean 333° is the correct bearing. The bearing is adjusted on the compass to correspond to the correct value. Now lay the edge of your compass on the map so that it crosses your chosen feature. Move the whole compass around this point until the orienteering lines on the compass are parallel with the south-north grid lines on your map, and pencil in a line. You are standing somewhere along this line. To determine exactly where, follow the same process using your second feature. The point at which your two lines intersect gives you your position.

> **To find your position using a compass:**
>
> – Choose two easily identifiable features on your map and the ground
> – Take a magnetic bearing from both
> – Deduct the magnetic variation to give grid bearings
> – Pencil in the lines on your map; the point at which they cross is your actual position.

USING MAP BEARINGS ON THE GROUND

When you know your position on a map you can use your map and compass to move over the ground to a predetermined point (for example, between A and B). Simply lay the edge of your compass between the two points, and adjust the turntable so that the orienteering lines on the compass lie parallel with the map's grid lines.

Read off the bearing at the base of the direction-of-travel arrow. This uses grid north and, needs to be converted to magnetic north before using it to walk by. Add the magnetic variation. If the grid bearing is 310° and the map error is 7° we will be walking on a bearing of 317°. Make this adjustment, then hold the compass at waist level, swivel your body until the magnetic needle is over the arrow and follow the direction-of-travel arrow to your destination.

Magnetic/grid north variation can be remembered with a simple mnemonic: MUGS (Magnetic Unto Grid, Subtract).

As with all areas of outdoor education, the only way to learn is to practice physically outdoors. Map-and-compass work is the most important skill, and poor technique kills many people each year. Never go beyond your capabilities. Survival means knowing when to stop, and using common sense.

Navigation on Land

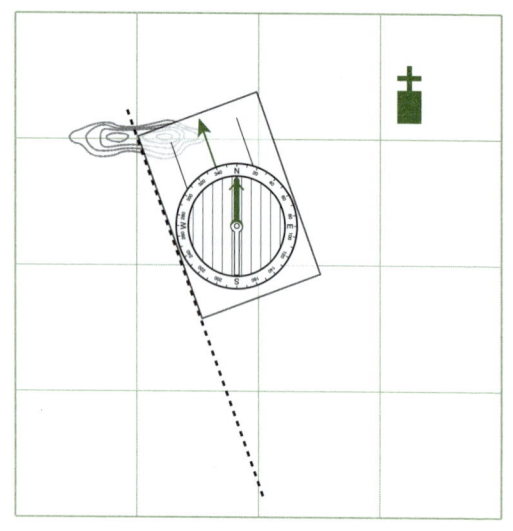

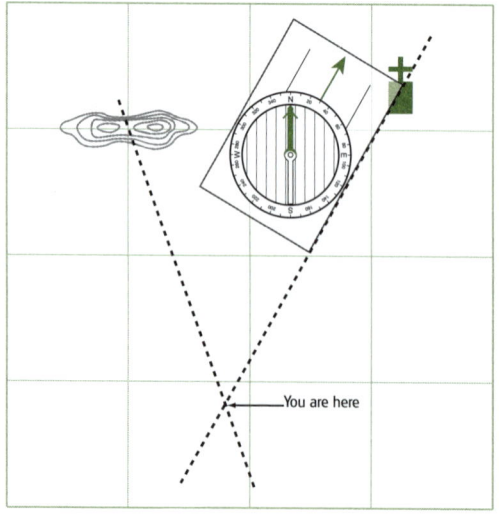

Finding your exact position on a map is easy to achieve with the aid of a compass

Navigation on Land

OCEAN NAVIGATION

Your chances of survival and rescue in ocean environments may depend on moving from your initial location – say to a more habitable island, or a busy shipping lane. To do so, you will need to navigate. This is straightforward with navigational instruments, but still possible with nothing at all. The most critical rule to remember is that the sun rises from an easterly direction but not directly east, and sets in a westerly direction, not due west. If you are in the Northern Hemisphere, the sun passes to the south of you; if you are in the Southern Hemisphere, it passes to the north of you.

To complicate things, from the Equator (0°) to latitude 23.5° north and 23.5° south, the sun's path varies – this is well known and logged, and determined by the time of the year. This variation must be accounted for when plotting any course.

DETERMINING CARDINAL POINTS

Away from equatorial zones, and ignoring any local daylight-saving time adjustments, the sun is due south at midday in the Northern Hemisphere, and due north at midday in the Southern Hemisphere. If you have a watch with an analogue dial, you can use this to determine direction. Set the watch to the current, local, unadjusted time, hold it horizontally and, in the Northern Hemisphere, point the hour-hand towards the sun. Now draw an imaginary line exactly half-way between the hour-hand and the 12 o'clock symbol. This is true south. In the Southern Hemisphere, point the 12 o'clock symbol at the sun, and true north lies midway between the hour-hand and 12 o'clock.

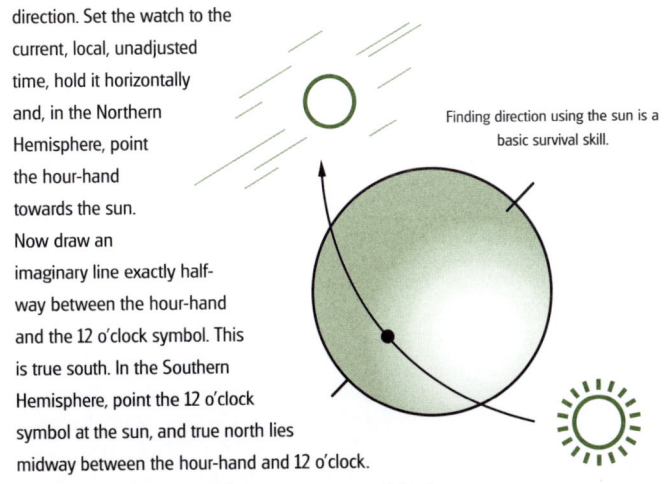

Finding direction using the sun is a basic survival skill.

If you do not have a watch or you are unsure of the time, you can determine the compass points and approximate time by planting a stick around a metre high in level, cleared ground. As the sun rises, mark the position of the stick's shadow, which will be cast to the west. During the day, watch the shadow's movement and length. The sun is at its highest at 12 noon, so the shadow will be shortest at mid-day and will point true north in the Northern Hemisphere and true south in the Southern Hemisphere.

At night, stars guide navigation. In the Northern Hemisphere, the North Star (Polaris) indicates true north. You can find it by following the front two stars of the constellation known as the Plough or Big Dipper (Ursa Major). In the Southern Hemisphere, the shaft of the Southern Cross (Crux) points to true south.

In many areas, the general wind direction is broadly constant; this is called the prevailing wind, and while it may vary from time to time, it is a good indicator of direction. These winds are most reliable where there are few obstacles to divert them, such as mountains, valleys and buildings.

Trade winds blow very steadily over the oceans and deserts in the tropics; they vary with the time of the year, but predominately blow towards the Doldrums at the equator. In the Northern Hemisphere they blow from the north-east, and in the Southern Hemisphere from the south-east. On land, winds that come from a constant direction often indicate the way to the coast. Looking how vegetation and plant life grows can also give a good indication of which direction the sea is in.

NATURAL INDICATORS

- Prevailing winds cause plants and trees to grow leaning away from them.
- Tall plant life has shorter growth on the windward side.
- Sand dunes have a gentler slope on the windward side.
- A build-up of sand and other debris behind plant life lies in the direction of prevailing wind.

Navigation on Land

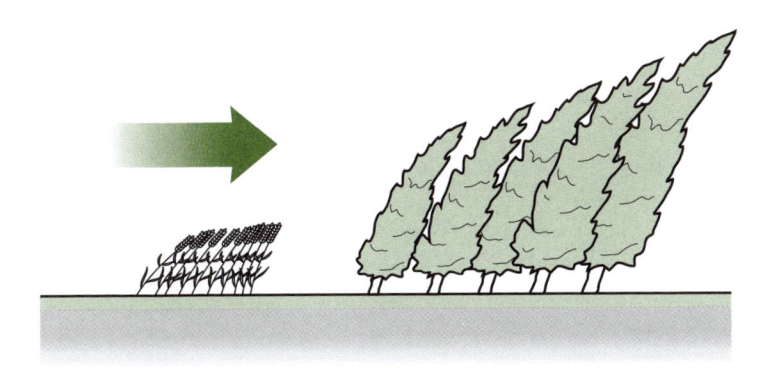

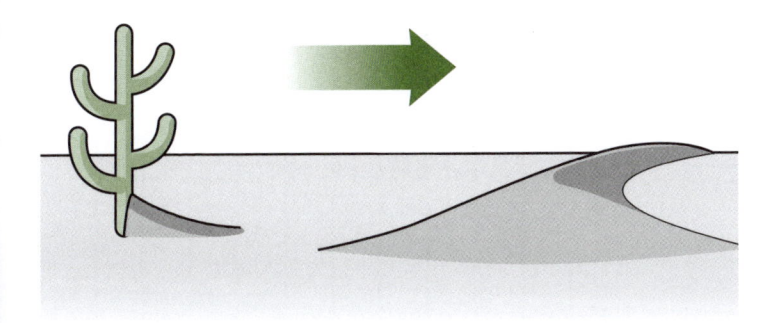

Use weather indicators to help you find your way: wind direction on trees (above) and sand dune sloping.

▲ Search and Rescue

There are many different designs of fire, each having a specific cooking, heating or water-purifying task. Some fires can be kept going for long periods, while others can be quickly extinguished and covered so as not to leave a trace of their existence.

If you become stranded, the chances are that the authorities will have initiated a search-and-rescue operation. The type of search depends on the area in which you are lost, the distances involved and the rescue equipment required for your particular problem.

In most cases when you are stranded because of an aircraft- or ship-related accident, the crew will already have transmitted the problem and location. Even if not, the vehicle will be fitted with emergency satellite-linked beacons. In these cases, your job is to survive until rescuers arrive. As this should not be too long, the best bet is to stay near the wreckage.

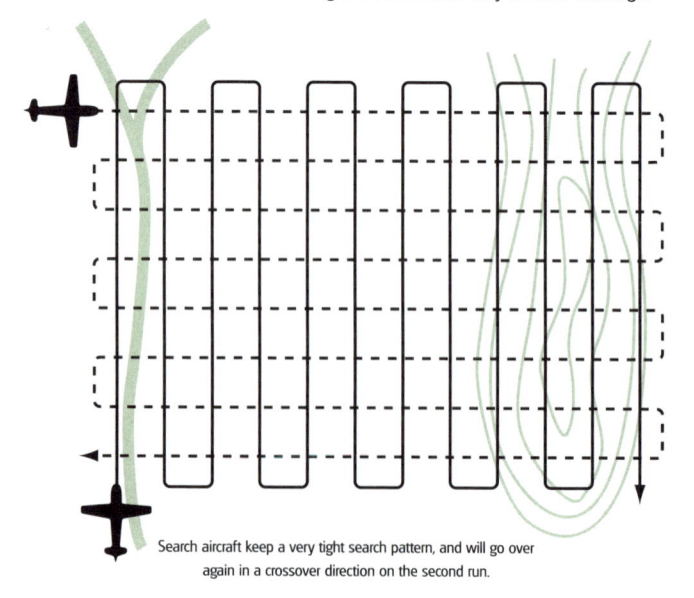

Search aircraft keep a very tight search pattern, and will go over again in a crossover direction on the second run.

If you were not travelling in a large vessel or aircraft, your exact position may not be known. The authorities will probably know your general whereabouts however, and will send out a search aircraft to pinpoint your position before sending a rescue party. Search aircraft will move in a definite pattern to ensure that they have covered the area properly.

Where aircraft are not used, teams of experienced searchers carry out the search, and may also bring specially-trained dogs with them. Sweep search is the most usual pattern, if the terrain is fairly flat with low vegetation. Teams search in line, members up to 20 metres apart, keeping visual contact. This may be a lot less in poor visibility. They move in a regular pattern too, and you will hear whistles as the team organises.

SELF-RESCUE

If there is little chance of being found, you may have to attempt self-rescue. This is a last resort – and even then requires a great deal of thought and planning. One crucial consideration is mode of travel. If you (or a fellow-survivor) know a great deal about navigating rivers, lakes and the sea, and you feel confident about the route, then you can think seriously about floating craft. Unfortunately, it is very difficult to build in escape contingencies for rafts and boats. Waterfalls and rapids (or storms) are major killers. This does not mean that you should not try, though; if you have looked at all the alternatives, and sailing is your decision, get on with it!

Often it is better to walk; almost everyone can do it. Dangers are usually pretty obvious. Remember that difficult terrain can be encountered at any time and place. In remote areas, you are more likely to encounter difficulties; they are remote for a reason. You need to be extra-careful and vigilant.

PLANNING A ROUTE

Negotiating snow and ice, moorland, scree or dense vegetation takes a great deal of time and energy. That means food. You must either have sufficient rations, or knowledge of appropriate local foraging skills. At rest, eating a handful of berries or a teaspoon of honey will boost your energy for 30 minutes or more; trekking, that same energy will last 30 seconds. You can conserve energy by planning your route. The shortest route is not necessarily best; a longer, simpler route can be quicker, safer and less tiring.

Good planning can alleviate hazards, or at worst will give you prior warning. This is obviously easier with maps, but you can take the high ground and see if you can pick a decent route visually. Either way, break the walk into small sections and study each one, noting potential problems and prominent features that can be seen from everywhere. If possible, identify any obvious linear features such as rivers or the edges of mountain ranges.

Try to keep the route at a constant height whenever possible, to conserve energy. Ascending and descending for no apparent reason demoralizes even the most experienced of walkers. Where this is impossible, choose slopes that are gradual and – if possible – scenic, to boost morale.

TIME AND MOTION

Hopefully, you will have a map. Having planned a route, you should work out the distance and the time. Plan to end the day well before nightfall, in as safe an area as possible. Leave time to prepare shelter and food. Note local dusk and dawn times.

Estimating time to distance is an important skill. Individuals have differing levels of pace and stamina, and in some locations – such as secondary jungle – you will be very lucky to manage a kilometre a day. However, there are guidelines.

Carrying a light pack

- 12 minutes per kilometre (0.6m), plus one minute for every 10 metres (10.9 yards) ascended
- On a map scale of 1:50,000, 1cm = six minutes; and one contour is 10 metres (10.9 yards) (1 minute)
- On a map scale of 1:25,000, 1cm = three minutes; and one contour is five metres (5.4 yards) (30 seconds).

Carrying a full pack

- 15 minutes per kilometre (.6m) + one minute per 10 metres ascended
- On a map scale of 1:50,000, 1cm = seven minutes; and one contour is 10 metres (one minute)
- On a map scale of 1:25,000, 1cm = four minutes; and one contour is five metres (30 seconds)

Search and Rescue

TRAIL-BLAZING

Only alter your plan in extreme need. Indicate changes from the agreed route with a definite trail-blazer's mark – cutting bark from trees, or marking direction arrows on the ground with heavy rocks or timber. This helps a following search party that may be aware of your proposed route – perhaps from evidence left at the crash site, or information from other survivors.

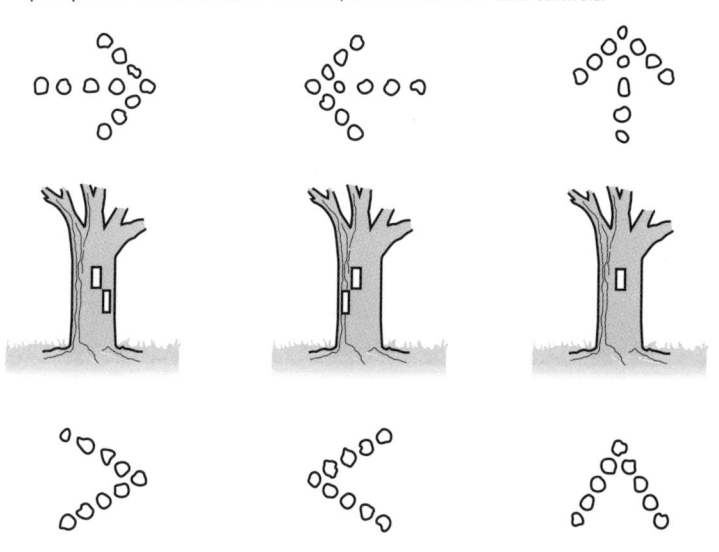

If you have decided to walk to safety, always leave easily followed indicators.

BRIEFINGS

Everyone involved in a self-rescue walk should know the exact route, aims and objectives, timings, difficulties and the reason behind any diversions. Groups hold together better with a clear leader; a second should also be appointed to take over in an emergency. Both should be experienced in navigation and walking, although if not they should at least have leadership qualities, especially confidence and a sense of humour. These key members must keep each other fully informed regarding the morale and health of the group.

Group briefing can happen well before the walkout, and any problems be ironed out in advance. Once the route is decided, all members can be given full details. Everyone involved – including anyone staying behind, or walking a different route – should have full knowledge of the plan, including written details if possible.

At this briefing, full details must be given about the people involved, people left behind and anyone taking another route. Any equipment, clothing, food and water should be distributed fairly, bearing in mind any given group's self-support opportunities. Overall safety and accident procedures – including agreed distress signals – should also be agreed. Flares should be distributed between the groups most likely to be able to discharge them. They are much more usable on open ground than in jungle, for instance.

GROUP DYNAMICS

There are always mixed abilities in any group, and this must be accounted for. The leader must recognize this fact and acknowledge it early in the briefing. Members daunted by the task need early reassurance.

Clothing and equipment should be decided on as soon as possible. If you have no appropriate clothing or equipment, it may not be worth the risk. If you do decide to go ahead, then use all the combined resources and give the best equipment to the walkers. People remaining behind will not need the toughest footwear, or water- and windproof clothing; they should have well-established shelters and fires. To walk over soft snow, you may have to make snow-shoes from wreckage or young, supple plant shoots.

You might have ropes, or be able to strip electric wiring from vehicle wreckage. If not, strip down vehicle interiors, cut material into long, thin strips and plait these together to make a safety rope. Originally, ropes were made from natural fibres – I have made strong, thin rope from twisting stinging nettle (Urtica dioica) stems together, and even thicker, longer ropes by splitting and twisting bramble (Rubus fruticosus) stems.

Having gathered together your clothing, equipment, food and water, you will have to carry it all. Once again, you can make carriers from wreckage, luggage or natural materials. Packs should be strapped to your back with the weight on your hips; the higher the pack sits, the better. Make sure that you pack so that you can get regularly-used items such as protective clothing without having to unpack the whole carrier.

GROUP MANAGEMENT

Once a self-rescue attempt begins, every member must watch out for all the others. If you are on your own, make absolutely sure that you do not endanger yourself. Getting

Search and Rescue

lost happens quite a lot. Once you realize you are lost, retrace your steps to a place you remember, and try again. Do not try to bluff the group. If you are lost, say so; even the most inexperienced group can see when something is wrong, and a competent leader is always honest.

Group discussion is the best way of approaching problems. Decide consensus actions. Never split up; that makes a difficult situation dangerous. Once a decision has been made, carry it through with confidence.

When you are hopelessly lost, head for a linear feature. Once you reach it, it will be much easier to decide which direction to proceed in, as there will be only two to choose from.

Always make a mental note of any prominent features – especially ones you identified at the planning stage. Sketching the area during planning is useful. As the group walks, members should look around – especially behind them. If anything goes wrong, they can use this visual knowledge to find their way back. If you are fortunate enough to have a compass, you should be constantly taking bearings to and from known features. Poor visibility can arise in minutes.

SURVIVING TRICKY NAVIGATION

When visibility hampers navigation – or you are forced on to featureless terrain and have to rely on the heavens for a bearing you can not take regularly – you can keep straight with a chain. This is done with three navigators working together. Start with the correct bearing. Three people form a line along that bearing so that the last can just see the first. The rearmost then walks to the front man and onwards, keeping his colleagues exactly aligned up. When he is as far as is safe, the new rearmost person then does the same, extending the line in the correct direction.

When sighting a distant feature, use one that isn't too far away. Heat from the ground can distort visual bearings. The same hold for bearings taken near large underground pipe works – which are often found in the desert – magnetic rocks, or during magnetic storms. Remain vigilant.

COMMON MISTAKES

When the group sets off, there is a tendency to force the pace. This must be avoided. Take a steady pace from the group's slowest member. Walkers out of breath soon tire, and weaker members drop back, becoming disheartened. Group morale suffers.

Search and Rescue

You may need to negotiate rock outcrops, especially at higher altitudes. Inexperienced walkers often speed up to reach the top, but what looks like the top rarely is; more often, there are several false peaks that can quickly sap energy and morale. Peaks are tiring and dangerous, but at least you are clearly visible from the air.

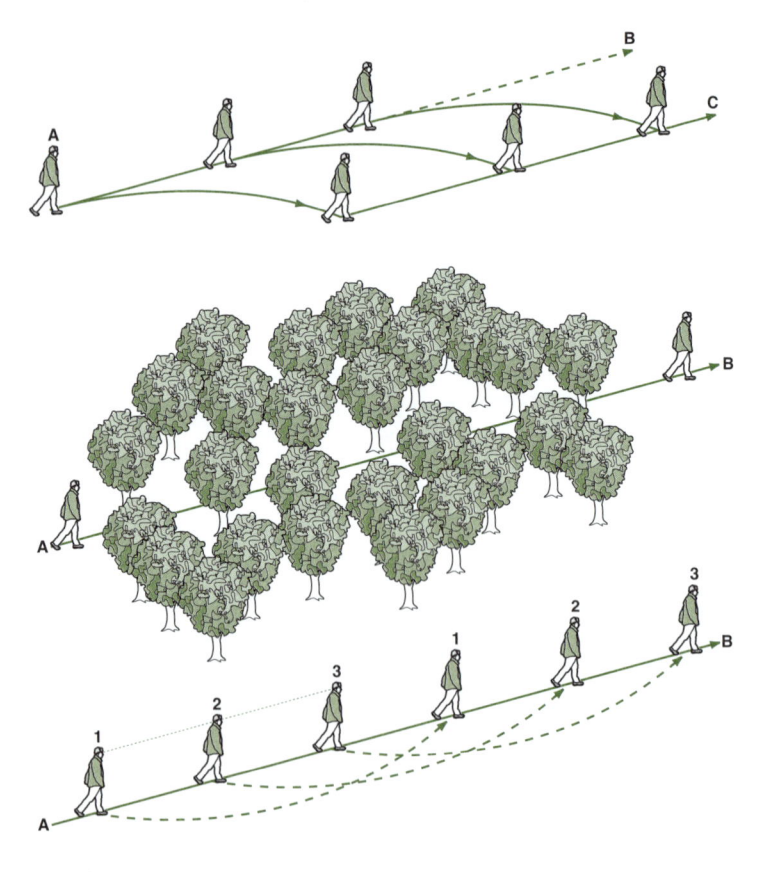

In featureless terrain or poor visibility, being able to keep to your planned route will depend on teamwork.

CLIMBING

Sometimes, you may have to climb. Ropes should ideally be available for protection, but not for climbing itself; rope is there to arrest a fall. Where climbing belts are not available, the climbers should be tied in with a single bowline knot. Never, ever tie to your clothing belt; it will never be strong enough. The safety rope should be controlled by a competent member, who is in turn secured by a belayer attached to the rope, which fastens to a secure anchor directly behind him in line. Very steep slopes down are best negotiated by abseiling, although this is a last resort and always requires good ropes.

CLASSIC ABSEIL TECHNIQUE

Abseiling involves sliding down a rope using friction to slow the rate of descent. The rope is used doubled and tied into a continual loop, then fastened around an abseil point, which may be a rock, tree or some other secure feature. In snow and ice, you may have to cut a snow bollard; this takes a lot of time, but may well be the only way to secure rope enough for abseiling or belaying. Bollards are mushroom shapes cut deep in the snow. The stalk must be at least one-and-a-half metres thick and half a metre deep. The rope is passed around this and must be insulated with packs or spare clothing as a friction guard to prevent it cutting the bollard. Tie the friction guard items to the rope. When everyone is down, the rope is then pulled through, along with the items.

If you do not have abseiling kit, you will have to use the classic method. Having secured the rope and tied the loose ends together, check that it reaches the ground or some other safe rest area, and that it is not caught or twisted. Stand astride the rope facing the anchor, and take the rope in front of you in the left hand and behind you in the right hand. Pull it up so that it touches your inside right thigh. Pass it around the right leg and diagonally across the chest and over the left shoulder. Keeping the left hand in place, grip the free hanging ropes behind you with your right hand again. Now move backwards a little at a time, turned slightly to the right and leading with the right leg, allowing the rope to slide around the body. To stop, pull the right hand and rope in front of the body – the extra friction will halt the descent.

The classic abseil is uncomfortable, and you should put some padding between the rope and your thigh. Take your time and keep your back straight. Avoid bending forward, as on a long abseil this can make breathing difficult. Two other methods – the sling and karabiner, and the Figure of Eight Descendeur – are a lot easier and less painful, but both need specific equipment.

SLING AND KARABINER ABSEILING

This method requires a sling that is twisted into a figure-of-eight shape. One leg should be placed through each of the loops, and a karabiner is then clipped on to the cross-section of the loops between the legs and to the front. The rope passes through the karabiner, then diagonally across the front of the body and over the shoulder; the rear hand holds the rope and controls the rate of descent.

FIGURE-OF-EIGHT DESCENDEUR ABSEILING

The figure-of-eight device incorporates small and large eyes in the shape of a figure eight. The doubled rope is fed through the large eye and then looped over the shank; the figure-of-eight is then attached to sling or climbing belt, using the small eye and karabiner, as described in the karabiner method. The rope then passes around the side of the body and to the rear, held by the right or left hand. You move the rear hand out to the side of the body to descend, and back to the rear to slow or stop.

Abseiling can also be used as a method of escape from situations such as burning buildings and aircraft.

Common Abseil Mistakes

- ▲ Because friction is the braking force in abseiling, you must be absolutely certain the rope is strong and resilient enough to withstand the strain. Many experienced mountaineers have lost their lives abseiling, and the following list records some of the causes:
- ▲ Anchor points not secure so ropes ride off
- ▲ Descent too fast, burning hands when trying to slow down
- ▲ Clothing and hair trapped
- ▲ Rope too short for the next safe stance
- ▲ Rope chopped by falling stone
- ▲ Abseiler knocked unconscious by falling stone
- ▲ Rope jammed around the anchor, stopping it from being retrieved
- ▲ Rope jams after clearing anchor so abseiler climbs back up and dislodges the loose rope
- ▲ Abseiler throws two ends of the rope over the cliff, but forgets to tie off
- ▲ Abseiler rests on a ledge part-way down the abseil; as he releases his weight, the elasticity of the rope causes a ripple to run up and flicks the rope off its anchor

Search and Rescue

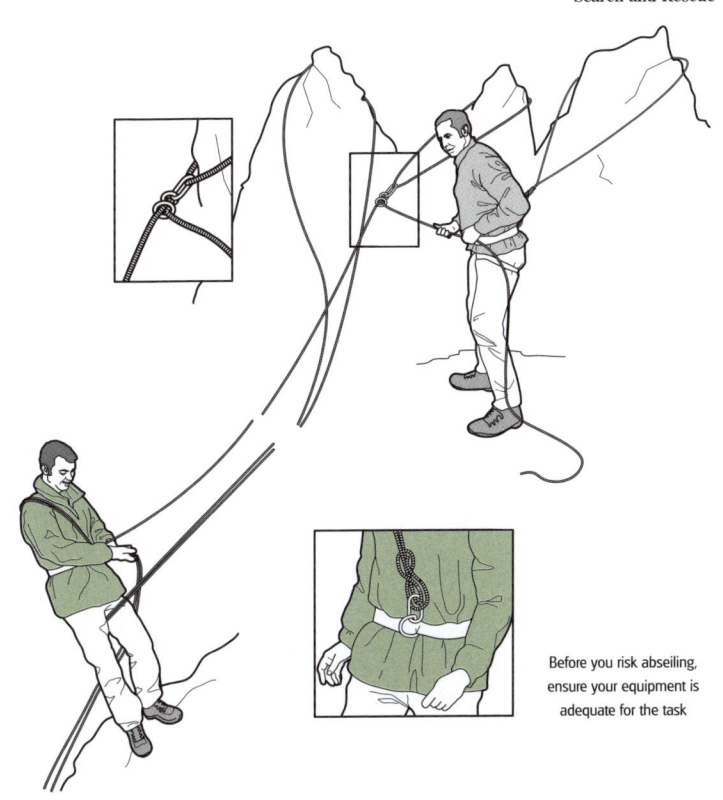

Before you risk abseiling, ensure your equipment is adequate for the task

MAINTAINING STAMINA

As a trek progresses, the group will need rest periods. Keep these short to avoid stiffness and coldness. In cold areas, the group should put on warm clothing as soon as they stop, and huddle together to share body heat. Any injuries will need tending. Footwear may be too tight, and adjusting socks might save blisters. Any hot spots need to be protected by smearing with animal fat or massaging the area. Usually five to ten minutes an hour is sufficient for tending needs. Drink plenty of liquid and eat small amounts regularly, to maintain stamina and morale. If food and water are scarce, keep pace and distance down until you can replenish both.

Soft ground, dense vegetation, scree, rocks, gullies and damp, slippery places are best avoided. They are dangerous and slow you down considerably. Where possible, use animal tracks, but remember they are used by animals, who may not be happy about having their territory intruded upon. In mountainous areas, if you cannot get lower down, use the ridges to avoid exhausting walking on sloping hillsides.

SENSIBLE WALKING

In remote areas without paths, walking groups should ascend and descend in single file. If there is a risk of dislodging loose rocks, walk abreast. On very steep, loose slopes, walk a zigzag pattern and keeping the group close so that if a rock is dislodged, it does not have the distance to gather enough speed to become dangerous. Where zigzags are impossible, move in small groups one at a time and wait on safe ground while the rest follow.

Regardless of your position or movement, if anything is dislodged, always assume there is someone lower down, and shout "Below!" as loudly as possible. It would be disastrous if you accidentally dropped a rock slide on an ascending rescue team.

Well-packed, short grass is by far the easiest ground to walk on, but can become very slippery on wet or icy hillsides – and walkers wearing waterproof clothing are almost frictionless if they fall. Descents are quicker on grass slopes, but only risk a direct route if there is a continual view to lower ground.

High grass and bracken make walking difficult and slow, so route around. Never use grass, bracken and small shrubs as hand-holds. They are shallow-rooted, and can lacerate your hands if your grip slips. Heather is also difficult to walk through. It clumps and can cover deep fissures. Be careful or you may shatter a leg.

Scree is a fast descent if you know how to walk on it, but it is also dangerous. The small rocks often shift without warning. Scree made from large chunks should be avoided as it takes a lot of energy to climb, and easily causes leg injuries.

Patches of soft, wet ground are normal in moorland. It is rarely dangerous, but best avoided as it is difficult to cross, and the wetness may cause trench foot. Similarly, go around streams, river and lakes if possible, or detour to a bridge. It is worth it.

Attracting Attention

You should always be ready to make your position known. Several noted survivors did not have signalling equipment available when potential rescue was nearby, and had to survive for many months before eventual rescue. Make sure you can attract attention from the moment you realize you are in trouble.

If there is vehicle wreckage, then spread it in a big patch in open country so it can be seen from the air. Shiny or bright items should go on high ground where they catch the sun and reflect light. If you are hidden because of thick vegetation, climb above the canopy and spread bright clothing and other materials on the trees. Try constructing a simple kite, and keep it flying.

If there is a river or stream, make a small raft, build a signal fire on it and float it downstream. Set it going at dusk. Even if the fire goes out, it will attract interest from any local who finds it.

In dense vegetation, the noise of approaching aircraft or other vehicles is deadened. If you are not prepared, you may not have time to signal, so keep devices close at hand.

If possible, keep a fire going. During the day, make the fire very smoky with fresh green leaves or engine oil. During darkness, create a clean, bright flame by burning petrol, aviation fuel or dry wood.

If you think other humans may be in the area, try shouting, ideally as a group. Face downwind. Voices do not carry through dense vegetation, so use a bit of wood to rhythmically beat a dead or hollow tree trunk instead.

⚠ International Distress Signalling

Using the official international distress signals makes it absolutely clear you are in trouble. Always carry a flashlight and whistle, even if they are small. When in distress, consider using the official signals. First, decide whether or not assistance is really needed. Ask yourself these two simple questions:

- ▲ **What are the implications if I do use a distress signal?**
- ▲ **What are the consequences if I don't?**

You may lose face – or be lightly fined – if you didn't need help, but you may die if you don't ask for it when needed! Therefore, do not be afraid to use standard international air-to-ground signals (shown opposite) if the situation warrants it.

Signalling tips

- **With a flashlight or vehicle light as signal, mask the light with a hand or jacket rather than switching it on and off, as this quickly drains batteries**
- **Noise is carried downwind. Turn your back to the wind for extra distance**
- **Keep signalling equipment close at all times**
- **If you are using flares, ensure there is nothing above you they can bounce off or be caught by**
- **Make ground-to-air signals as large and clear as possible**
- **Using Morse Code to signal SOS (... --- ...) is only a good idea if you can read a Morse answer. If you are signalled back but do not respond, rescuers may think it is a hoax**
- **Once you contact rescuers, keep signalling until you know they can actually see you**
- **If you ever signal and then are forced to move site, make sure you trail-blaze**
- **If you signal and then manage self-rescue, tell the authorities immediately so they can call off rescue operations.**

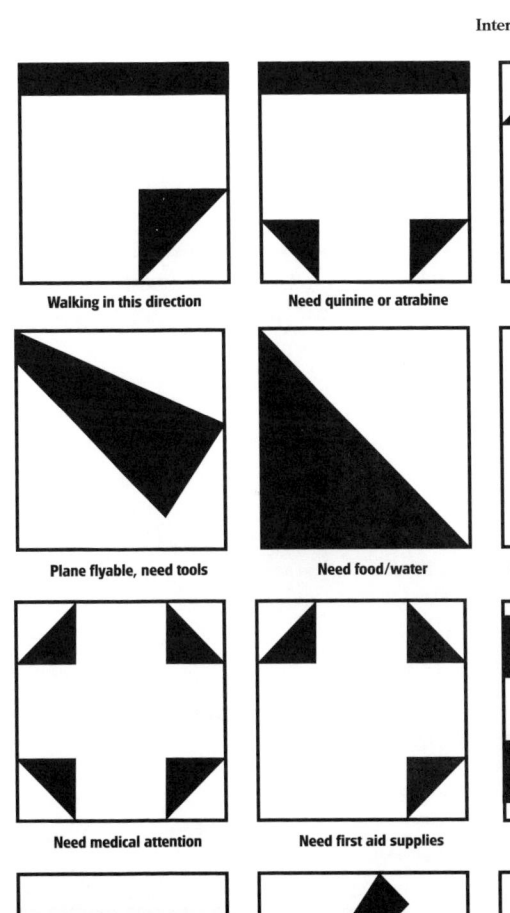

International Distress Signalling

Walking in this direction	Need quinine or atrabine	Need warm clothing
Plane flyable, need tools	Need food/water	Need fuel and oil. Plane flyable
Need medical attention	Need first aid supplies	Show direction to civilisation
Should we wait for rescue plane	OK to land arrow shown direction	Do not attempt landing

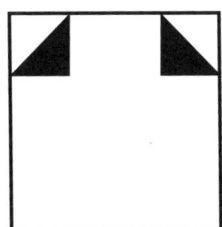

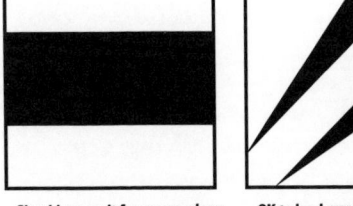

▲ The Body's Needs

We take water for granted. The body requires daily fluid to maintain its everyday functions, and soon becomes inefficient without it. Dehydration causes exhaustion – and further dehydration – and then kidney failure. Death occurs quickly afterwards. Once the kidneys fail, there is no hope in a survival situation, and even expert medical care gives only a slim chance.

It is vital you drink water regularly. You can go without food for 20 or 30 days, but without water, you are lucky to last six. In my experience, even three days without water results in serious effects – including severe headaches and such exhaustion that even seeking liquid becomes near-impossible.

Even in temperate climates, you need one and a half litres of water a day. In hot climates, this increases to a minimum of six litres. However, it is possible to survive temporarily on as little as 250 ml. To do this, you must reducing sweating – sleeping and resting during the day, especially in hot climates. Keeping your mouth closed and breathing through your nose also helps.

WATER SHORTAGES

When water is short, taking care of personal hygiene and ensuring clean food preparation helps avoid sickness and diarrhoea – the biggest causes of body fluid loss in a survival situation. Cigarettes, alcohol and caffeine dehydrate you too, so hold off! Alcoholic drinks should be poured into shallow containers and placed in a solar still to extract the water. The resulting neat alcohol can be used for sterilisation. Water is also needed to digest food, so cut back on food intake to maintain fluid levels. When you do eat, there are two rules you should keep in mind:

- ▲ **Foods high in carbohydrates, such as sugars and starches, require only a minimum amount of water for digestion, and fruit and veg often have high water content.**
- ▲ **Protein foods such as meat, fish, eggs – and especially seaweed – require large amounts of water to process. Avoid them.**

▲ **Although we often feel thirsty, this is not a good indicator of the body's true need for water. Do not drink just because you feel thirsty; monitor your water intake instead: You can alleviate thirst by sucking a button, pebble or something similar.**

Do not drink sea water, as the high salt content makes it a dehydrator. However, you can extract water from it with a solar still and the resulting salt crystals can be saved to maintain the body's salt balance. Drinking urine may seem necessary, but in fact urine is one of the ways the body removes waste products from the system. Reintroducing them leads to kidney failure. Urine, too, can be processed in a solar still.

If you are relying on solar stills, you will have to ration water, but do so only in extreme circumstances. The regime I favour is the following:

Water rationing schedule

- **Day one: water only for the injured**
- **Days two to four: 0.7 pints (400ml) per person**
- **Day five onwards: 0.17 to 0.5 pints (100–300ml) issued daily per person**

This is far from ideal, but at least it will maximize your chances of survival. If you can maintain the following water intake, you should not have any problems:

Degrees C / F	Pints (Litres) per 24h
25° / 77°	1.7 (1.0)
30° / 86°	3.4 (2.0)
35° / 95°	8 to 10 (5.0–6.0)

THE SOLAR STILL

In hot areas with little rainfall, you will need to make a solar still. This is not ideal, but it does work if built correctly. It functions by condensing water vapour on to a surface. This condensation is then collected into a container for drinking. The idea came from First World War soldiers, who slept under

The Body's Needs

their rubberized gas capes and noticed that the capes got wet underneath. A solar still can be a life-saving piece of equipment capable of producing a few hundred mls of water a day, but it needs careful siting and construction.

Dig a round hole 1.5 to two feet (60–70cm) deep and five feet (150cm) wide with your collection container in the bottom-centre of the hole. If you have one, put the collector in a tray or bigger container. Ideally, run a tube or straw from the container base to the outer edge so you can extract water without disturbing the still. Stretch a piece of polythene, canvas or waterproof material over the hole and mound earth heavily around the circumference. Place a stone or similar in the centre of the sheet so it sags into a cone over the container. Metal also works if the right shape.

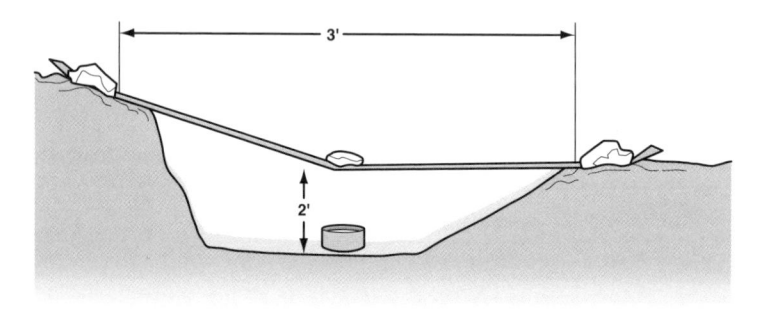

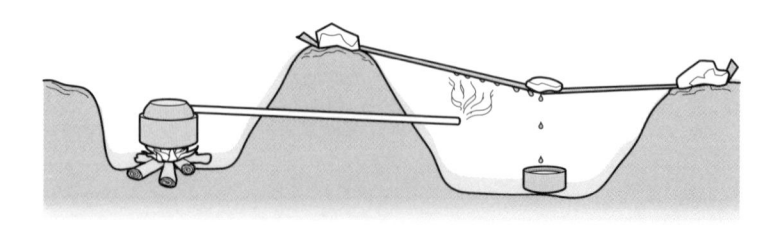

(Top) The solar still should be constructed with care and ideally sited in a location where water vapour is naturally present. (Above) Piping in steam from a kettle in an adjacent hole will enhance water production.

OPTIMISING SOLAR STILLS

Solar stills work because the sun heats the air and soil of the still, evaporating any water in there. Once evaporation begins, the vapour precipitates on the material and the droplets eventually run down the cone and drip into the container. You collect more if the underside of the material is as rough as possible. It helps if you have green vegetation to put in the bottom of the hole.

If you have clean sources available – salt water, natural water, alcoholic drinks – put just those in the tray or empty them into the bottom of the still. If you have no clean source, use any foul water available, such as urine, engine water, animal bladders or stagnant pond water. Distilled clean water is safe to drink immediately. If any foul water was present, the collected water must be purified first.

Constructing a still in dry river beds, areas with bedrock and natural depressions improves the chance of a good supply. The more stills you build, the better your chance of collecting enough water to survive.

You can also carefully dig a second hole next to the still and light a fire in it, then put a kettle of liquid on the fire and run a pipe from it through the wall and into the still. This steam will condense normally and greatly enhance water production. You may be able to make a kettle from wreckage, or use a large bamboo piece as the pot with small bamboo pieces as the pipe. Keeping the fire very low will mean all steam is collected rather than wasted, and also preserves the kettle's lifespan.

PURIFYING WATER

Never assume water is safe to drink: unless you are certain of its cleanliness, take no chances. Many outdoor and travel shops sell filter straws that clean the water as it passes through. These do not cost much, and should be added to your first-aid kit and all travel bags. Halazone tablets are excellent for cleansing water, although they can be dangerous if you don't use them properly. If you have no equipment at all, you must boil the water to kill harmful bacteria. Water must be boiled for at least 15 minutes to purify it. In absolute emergency, water from a solar still is safer than raw foul water, so that should be your minimum protection, but solar stills do allow plenty of dangerous contaminants through.

LOCATING WATER

Your first concern should be to watch the sky. You can usually see rain or snow approaching. Rainwater and snow are safe to drink – although poisonous vegetation and bacteria from

The Body's Needs

dirty containers and collecting equipment may contaminate the water. Always have as many containers as possible ready to catch the rain. You cannot have too much fresh water.

Solar stills will collect rainwater too, but will need emptying throughout the downpour to prevent collapse. If all else fails, use clothing and material to soak up rainfall and either suck the water from the clothing or wring it out to top up supplies.

PLANT WATER

Remember that all green vegetation needs water to live. Green plants release excess water as vapour from leaves – often lots of it. You can cut a deep 'V' shape into a tree and collect its sap as it rises, the same way as rubber is tapped. Both birch and aspen can produce lots of drinkable sap. With unfamiliar trees, put the sap in a solar still and treat as foul water. Avoid drinking directly from a tree you do not know to be safe; if the sap is milky or discoloured, assume it is toxic, and do not even handle it.

If you have polythene bags or similar – cabin crew often carry a supply of rubber gloves, for example – then put them around leaves and tie them. You will collect evaporated water. Even a light waterproof jacket or other waterproof material will collect dew if you lay it on grass or dense vegetation; turn it over carefully to keep the water in place, and you can mop it off, or funnel the water into your reservoir.

Many plants trap water which can be collected and purified. In the jungle, you can drink from many of the vines without purifying. The floor-level end of the vine holds most of the water, up to about a metre off the ground. Cutting above this point without disturbing the rest will allow you to drink the cool, fresh water without losing any. As with trees, vines with milky or very discoloured liquid should be left alone. Bamboo also has a good supply of clean, easy water. It is held between the bamboo segments. Cutting into these segments releases the water.

FROZEN WATER

Sea ice over a year old has no noticeable saltiness, as the salt particles sink to the bottom of the ice. Sea ice over three years old is generally fresher than most rivers, while old sea ice can be distinguished by its rounded corners and its bluish tint. Icebergs are similar, but extremely dangerous to approach or move around on.

Snow and ice should be melted to provide fresh water. If using a container over a fire, put a little in at a time and wait for it to melt fully before adding to it. Do not compress snow in a container and place it on a heat source; the snow will melt at the base of the pan, but the rest will insulate the pan bottom and it will burn through. Do not suck ice or snow, either. Your mouth will get frozen, and you risk choking if the ice becomes stuck in your throat.

Be aware that no natural water freezes completely. You may be able to break nearby ice and collecting the water below. Snow insulates ice from cold: the deeper the snow, the shallower the ice. When collecting water from snow-covered ice, be very careful that you do not fall through the ice.

LOCATING WATER SOURCES

In summer, water can be collected from streams, rivers and pools. Do not take water from the edges, as debris collects there. When you cannot locate a water supply, you can use animal and insect life to lead you to water. They all need water to live, although they can drink foul water without coming to any harm and their sources will need purifying.

If you see a line of ants or other communal insects, follow it until you find their water source. Birds, especially seed-eaters, need a lot of water, so watch how they are flying. In vegetation, birds flying fast and low without stopping are probably going toward water, whereas if they are flying from branch to branch they are usually full of water and are coming away from the source.

If you can, find an animal that is unlikely to attack you and trap it without killing it. Tie a long lead around its neck and stake it out overnight. The following day, release it, keeping hold of the lead, and let it wander where it wants to. At first, it will attempt to evade you, but eventually it will settle down and thirst will drive it to its watering place. Once it has led you to the water, kill it for your next meal.

At the shoreline, underground fresh water meets heavier salt water – usually on the landward side of dunes. Dig until your hole fills with water, then stop digging, and allow the water to settle sufficiently to allow the sediment and the salt water to sink to the bottom. This may take several hours. When it has settled, use your hand or a shallow container to skim the top layer off the water. If it is salty, dig again, further back and deeper. Continue until you find fresh water. All water from the ground tastes earthy and brackish, even after purification. However, you do get used to the taste eventually.

FILTERING WATER

In a survival situation, your water will not come in the clean, fresh state you are used to. Making a filter helps sift out debris. On the seashore, you can pass the water through a

The Body's Needs

container of broken shells and tiny pebbles. In other locations, straw or heather will suffice. If you have spare clothing or bandages, these can also be used. Avoid wool unless there is absolutely no alternative; I speak from experience here, and although it works, it tastes awful! No matter how well your filter works, the water still must be purified, even before you wash foodstuffs in it.

QUICK WATER TIPS

- ▲ If you suspect water may be a problem, carry enough for your entire journey
- ▲ Where water is stored for emergency use, check and change it regularly
- ▲ Do not assume that water is safe to drink
- ▲ If there is any doubt about water quality, purify it
- ▲ Do not use unpurified water to clean your teeth, or to wash your mouth or food
- ▲ Do not drink sea water, urine, blood or the clear liquid found around the eyes of animals and fish
- ▲ Conserve your own body's water as much as possible
- ▲ Ration only in the most extreme circumstances
- ▲ When extracting water from vegetation and trees, do not drink any that is milky or dark in colour.

▲ Cooking Fires

You can live without food for a considerable time, but you need it in the long term for energy and the short term for body heat. Food and drinks are much more palatable hot, but even cold food produces inner heat.

Lighting a fire and keeping it going is not easy; it takes patience and effort, but it is very important. You can cook with it, warm yourself directly, heat warming stones to place inside your shelter and bedding, boost morale and confidence enormously and keep away dangerous animals.

A cooking fire can be used in different ways. If you are boiling or griddling food on a tray or wreckage piece, the fire should encourage flames; if spit-roasting, toasting or baking, it should have hot embers with little or no flame at all.

MATCHES AND CIGARETTE LIGHTERS

The first part of fire-lighting is arranging a method of ignition. Petrol-filled cigarette and cigar lighters are ideal – gas-fuelled lighters tend to freeze at altitude – but obviously run out sooner or later. Good matches have a strong wooden stem, while cheaper ones are made from rolled paper, plastic or card and often break or burn out very quickly. Household matches are useless when damp. You can dry slightly damp matches a little by running them through your dry hair several times before striking carefully, using as little force as possible. Beyond slightly damp, do not even try; it is better to let them dry naturally. They may still become usable eventually.

Survival-conscious enthusiasts create waterproof matches for travel bags. These should be sturdy, red-headed 'strike anywhere' matches. Dripping wax from a candle to seal the whole match will do the job. Coating the match with varnish (even nail varnish) takes a long time, but it stays in place until scraped away, whereas wax will melt and run in heat. Keep such matches in a waterproof container; a plastc 35mm film canister holds many matches and is easily sealed. Standard-size matches are short enough to leave space in the cannister for some cotton wool for tinder.

CANDLES

You need to conserve ignition sources as much as possible, and lighting a candle gives you a tool to start a slow-catching fire without burning through all your matches or lighters. If you do

Cooking Fires

not have any candles, make a faggot of wood by bundling small twigs tightly together. Once it has been lit, its tightness keeps it going for quite some time. The initial flames often give way to smouldering, further slowing down the burning process; blow on to the embers and the flames will reappear.

You can manufacture candles using string as a wick and moulding animal fat around it. These are nowhere near as good as commercial wax ones, but in a long-term survival situation, using them to light your fires will save the life of your matches, your lighters and, possibly, yourself.

BATTERIES

Without matches or lighters, creating an ignition source is down to sheer determination. If you have a vehicle battery, then you can use this to start a fire; the bigger the battery, the better. Attach heavy wire to the terminals, and touch the ends of the wires together. Be very careful; if the wire is too light, it will melt and either way, the wire will become hot and can burn you. There is also the risk of an electric shock. This even works with ordinary household batteries as used in toys, flashlights and other items; stretch a strand of wire wool between the terminals, hold it in place with bits of rock or wood, and use the heat generated as the wire wool melts.

THE BURNING LENS

The sun can be an endless source of ignition. The sunnier the day, the better; during overcast, there is no chance of lighting a fire with the sun. Turning sunlight into fire involves concentrating the sun's rays. You use a glass lens to concentrate the sun on to your tinder until it ignites; magnifying-glass lenses are ideal for this, and work very quickly, but spectacles can also be used, and even broken glass, or a glass container filled with water.

Another good method is to use a cone-shaped mirrored surface to concentrate the power. The most effective device is a flashlight lens. Remove the bulb and place very dry, easily ignited tinder such as loose cotton wool at the base of the lens. Angle it so that the sun is shining straight into it and keep it pointed exactly at the sun.

FLINT AND STEEL

Many outdoor shops sell purpose-made flint and steel firelighters. These consist of an oversized cigarette lighter flint and a small section of hacksaw blade. The blade is run down the flint, raining hot sparks on to your tinder: very simple but very effective. You can get the

Cooking Fires

Burning glass

Flint and steel

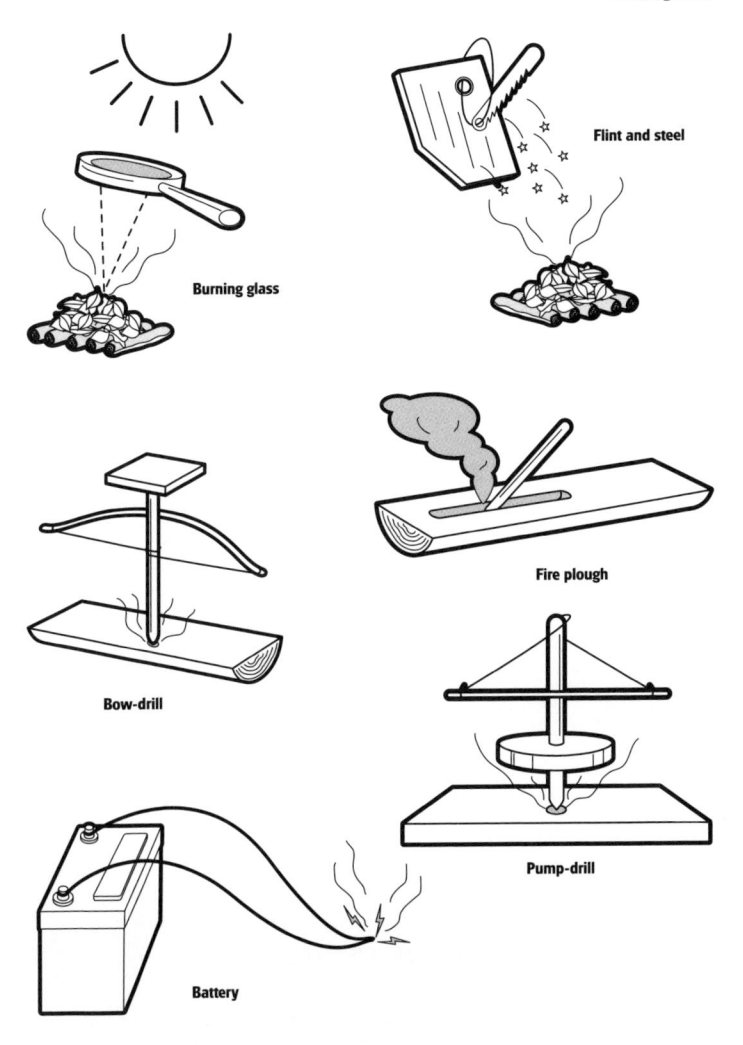

Bow-drill

Fire plough

Pump-drill

Battery

In the absence of matches and lighters, igniting fires is a time-consuming business. Everything must be ready and waiting before you begin to ignite the tinder.

Cooking fires

same result much less efficiently by hitting a piece of flint stone with a knife.

WOOD ON WOOD

If you must rely on the environment to provide your fire-lighting equipment, expect to use a great deal of time, effort and muscle power. Using friction to produce heat is difficult, but becomes easier with practice. Essentially, you have to produce enough friction to heat a piece of wood to burning point. You must prepare well. Make sure that the wood is as dead and as dry as possible. It helps enormously if you use a hardwood for the moving piece (male) and a softwood for the recipient (female), as this maximises friction. Eventually, you will produce enough heat to start a fire. Carve a hollow in the softwood from both sides, so that only a thin wafer of wood is left. The paper-thin wood becomes an ember much sooner. Adding tinder and blowing carefully then produces a flame.

Bamboo can also be used. Split a dead piece down the centre, and, using one half, cut a hole – making sure that the edges are shaved thin. Take a long strand of thin bamboo that fits neatly into the hole, and saw it across the hole. Once again, the more friction, the quicker the ignition.

THE BOW-DRILL

In a piece of dry softwood, dig a round hollow in a conical shape at the edge and half-way through the timber. Turn the softwood over and carve a second hollow to meet the first, making sure that there is a feather of thin wood between the hollows. Put the broad end of the male piece into the hollow and draw the bow back and forwards to rotate the hardwood male piece.

The process is quite easy; the main difficulty is gauging the amount of pressure to achieve maximum friction without the male piece sticking. As soon as the softwood ignites, remove the hardwood and blow into it while holding a little fine, dry tinder against the ember, until it bursts into flame.

THE PUMP-DRILL

The effort of making a pump drill can be well worth it. The male timber should be about three feet (1m) in length, carved into a taper from one inch (3cm) in diameter at the top to two inches (5cm) three-quarters of the way down its length, and finishing with a slight point at the tip. Carve a notch diagonally across the top of the male piece one inch (2cm) deep and 0.25 inches (0.5cm) wide.

The next stage is to carve a flywheel from a piece of tree trunk or branch about 12 inches

(30cm) in diameter and 3–4 inches (8–10cm) thick. Carve a 1.5 inch (4cm) hole in the centre of the segment. If you cannot cut a piece off the trunk, you can use a heavy log six inches (15cm) thick and one foot (30cm) long. The flywheel should fit over the male piece and stick as the timber widens. Tighten it by tapping it down. Take a green, fresh piece of timber 1.5 feet (0.5m) long and four inches (10cm) in diameter, and carve a hole half-way down its length at the midway point, tying a strong piece of string at the ends; this is the pump section. Place this hole over the top of the male piece, with the string seated in the carved groove. Adjust the string so the pump stops a little above the flywheel.

Place the male into the female as described in the bow drill method. With one hand, hold the pump and turn the male so that the string twists around it until the pump lifts to near the top of the male. Now put both hands on the pump and push sharply down. The string unwinds and straightens, quickly turning the male and throwing the flywheel around. When the string fully unwinds, stop pressing down so the flywheel can continue on its journey – lifting the pump back to the top of the male as the string twists around it again. Continue with this action until you hit burning point.

PREPARING A FIRE

You must prepare your fire before igniting. Poor preparation is the quickest way to exhaust ignition sources. An outdoor fire requires a lot of fuel in three distinct stages.

The first is the tinder, best described as easily combustible material; the better the tinder, the easier the lighting procedure. Fine, open material such as fluffed-up cotton-wool is ideal, especially if impregnated with an accelerant such as petrol. You can ignite this with little trouble. The more you have, the better; as a minimum, you will need enough to fill a soccer ball.

If you do not have good-quality tinder available, you will have to find some. Very fine shavings from dry softwoods will do. Birch trees produce very good tinder if you peel and use the paper-thin bark. Dry leaves and grasses will help. If you can find an empty bird's nest, the lining makes an excellent starter, progressing to the main nest as the flame builds.

KINDLING

You'll need a good-sized site for the main fire. The second stage requires as large a pile of kindling as possible – enough to fill a medium-sized tent. This may sound excessive, but it is the very minimum required for establishing a fire enough to take the larger fuel

Cooking Fires

you need for warmth, cooking and boiling water. Kindling is made up of materials such as thin dead twigs and strips of old bark – nothing thicker than a pencil. If wood is scarce, you will have to make do with what you can find. In snow-covered regions, you will have to dig to find your materials.

Arrange a small pyramid of kindling mixed with tinder, leaving a small opening for the ignition source. Do not put too much kindling on in the first place, as the fire will become oxygen-starved. This is especially true when too much grass and and too many leaves are used; they flare up spectacularly, but then die away leaving a mound of ashes that saps oxygen and stops the fire. Adding kindling a little at a time encourages a good, hot fire.

Once the kindling is lit and burning productively – a minimum of smoke and a maximum of flame – the third stage takes place. This entails adding larger, heavier timber to the fire, anything from pieces four inches (10cm) in diameter to full-grown tree trunks if you can carry them! Bigger pieces burn for a long time and keep the fire going. Keeping a fire going requires an enormous amount of fuel; a pile of timber a metre high and two metres in diameter will only last a day, maybe two at most if you conserve the fuel by adding just a little each time the fire begins to die.

At this stage, you can keep the fire going as long as you have fuel. I have kept fires going with rain pouring down by covering the fire with a layer of logs topped with earth, and then uncovering it when the rain has passed.

SITING YOUR FIRE

Choose a flat, sheltered place where the fire cannot easily spread. Clear the ground of vegetation. If it is wet or covered with snow and ice, build a loose raft layer from logs and make the fire on this. Dig a trench to put the fire in if there is no other shelter from wind. Have space to keep all your fuel close to hand, so you can build and tend the fire without having to leave. A platform for the fire to rest on and a surround to keep it contained both help, but never use rocks or stones from riverbeds or wet places, as these absorb water and will explode when hot. If it seems too wet or windy, trust yourself and wait for better weather, saving your resources.

Fires and caves never go well together, but if there is no choice, the fire should be at the rear. The heat will take most of the smoke to the roof, where it can be sucked outside along the roof. It will still be very smoky, however. The mouth of the cave is even worse, though; when the wind blows your way, the whole cave will fill with smoke and sparks. A wind-break wall behind the fire may shelter it from wind and can act as a heat reflector, but rock walls can topple onto the fire and knock burning logs in, and log walls may themselves catch fire.

If you have big sheets of metal wreckage, lay pieces together to make a long metal bed on the ground and cover most of the length with a few centimetres of earth. Building your fire on the exposed end will heat the whole bed, giving you under-floor heating, especially if your shelter is on the other end. Make sure the bed is long enough that you are safely away from the fire.

FUEL

Have all your wood ready in advance. Gather a soccer ball's-worth of tinder to light the fire, and keep it dry until you are ready; putting it under clothing helps. Then gather at least a good tent's-worth of kindling, none of which should be thicker than a pencil. Finally, if you have time, get a day's-worth of timber; a heap three feet (1m) tall and six feet (2m) in diameter. Several logs are the minimum; they will give you time to find more fuel. Once the fire is going well, even wet timber burns. When collecting, look in trees and bushes; dead timber even a few inches off the ground is a lot drier than anything on the ground.

Finding fuel becomes a major preoccupation in survival situations. If you manage to collect enough to stockpile, stand it upright, either resting it against a tree or rock or by building it into a bonfire shape; the rain will run off the steep surface and not soak through.

Other fuels are possible. These include coal (usually found just under the surface), peat (cut into small blocks and dried for a couple of days first), and sticky tar substances (usually found in limestone areas). Animal fats and dung also work; the fat burns easily, but dung needs to be dried; gather it in dead vegetation and stack it off the ground to let the air dry it out.

IGNITION

Conserve matches or cigarette lighters by lighting a candle or faggot to ignite the fire with. Once the fire is alight, make every effort to keep it going; letting it go out is unacceptable. Conserve fuel by using it little and often. Use earth to dampen the fire, removing it to bring it back to life when you need the extra warmth, or for cooking and purifying water. Be ready to cover the heart of the fire when rain or snow threatens it.

TYPES OF FIRE

There are many different designs of fire, each having a specific cooking, heating or water-purifying

Cooking Fires

function. Some fires can be kept going for long periods, while others can be quickly extinguished and covered so as not to leave a trace of their existence. Fires can burn without the slightest amount of smoke, giving a pure flame that shines brightly as a night-time signal and provides ideal water-boiling power, while others can be made to give off thick clouds of smoke, detectable for miles around during daylight hours – important for daylight signalling and for smoking and preserving food. The type of fire you construct will depend on the food you need to cook and the environment in which you find yourself.

THE PIT FIRE

Ideal for windy conditions. Roll back a section of turf and dig out a half-metre pit. A raft of timber at the bottom will stop dampness from threatening the initial fire. Heat cannot escape from the sides so pits retain heat well, and are especially good for cooking with limited fuel. The concentrated heat keeps the embers very hot, ideal for spit-roasting. Because the fire is below ground level, you can improvise cooking lines and boiling pans without any elaborate framework. Once finished with, the fire can be easily concealed by back-filling it and unrolling the turf. Pit fires are little use for heating or signalling at night, and require constant tending to keep going for long periods.

A) Turf rolled back

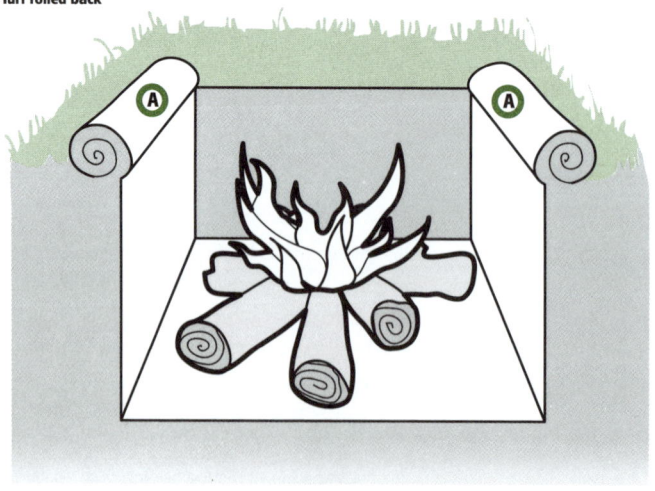

Cooking Fires

THE PYRAMID FIRE

Dig a broad, shallow trench, and use the edges to build a simple green timber pyramid, keeping the fire low so the timbers do not burn very quickly. Placing a decent-sized flat stone or piece of metal on top gives you a very effective hot-plate – ideal for melting animal fat and frying food. Do not use a stone from near a river, stream or damp place, as it will explode violently. This fire is not a great deal of use for night-time signalling.

A) Stone plate

Cooking Fires

POACHER'S BOILING FIRE

Good for boiling, purifying water and generating signal light. Build a circular fire and lay two large pieces of fresh green timber in a 'V' shape, with the fire in the middle of the 'V' and the opening positioned into the prevailing wind. Use three long, fresh, green timbers to form a high tripod-shape over the fire, using timber with a natural spur as a pan-hanger. Hang your pan over the fire. Lay plenty of dry fuel directly below the pan. The wind funnelled by the 'V' will soon fan the fire to high flames – ideal for boiling. To regulate the flames a little, reposition the 'V' with the point into the wind.

POACHER'S GRIDDLE FIRE

If you have no pot, this fire lets you fry or bake food. Build a circular fire. You then need a long pole of fresh, green timber and another piece of timber with a natural spur to act as a pole rest. Attach a decent-sized flat, dry stone to the long pole, and use it as a cooking plate. You can either keep the plate in the same position throughout the cooking process by placing a large rock to secure it, or you can adjust the height over the fire to speed up or slow down the cooking. Once the food is cooked, all you need to do is lift the plate out of the fire and you can eat straight off it.

Three sides of fire

Think of a fire as a triangle with three sides: heat, fuel and oxygen. If one side is removed the triangle will collapse, causing the fire to go out.

Cooking Methods

Different cooking methods help vary the survival diet, aiding morale. Proper cooking also makes the foods more palatable and reduces the risk of food poisoning. Wherever possible, wrap your food in aluminium foil or cook it in a container to reduce shrivelling and to conserve juices. Baking in firm mud is also excellent; completely cover the food with a thick layer, and let it dry before placing it in the embers of the fire or digging it in under the fire. If there is plenty of dried grass, wrap the food in the grass. Give the parcel enough time for the mud to be baked hard all the way through before removing it from the heat.

Roasting meat, fish and root vegetables on a spit is another good option. A roasting fire should have embers, not flames, or else the food will burn on the outside and stay raw inside. Rotate the food to ensure proper cooking, and be patient; it is a slow process. If your spit is wooden, use strong, green timber to reduce the chance of it burning through.

Smoking food gives it a pleasant alternative taste and preserves it. Quick smoking leaves a thin layer of carbon on the outside, but does not preserve the inside. To preserve the food thoroughly, smoke it slowly over days, allowing the carbon to penetrate deep into the flesh. Only use hardwoods for smoking fuel, as the smoke from softwood can cause cancer. If in any doubt, the safest way to cook food is to dice it into very small pieces and boil it.

COOKING CRUSTACEANS

Crustaceans should be boiled. They require only a little cooking time, and once caught must be cooked and consumed quickly, as they will soon begin to go off.

COOKING FISH

All cooking methods work for fish. Freshwater fish are better when boiled for a short time to remove the earthy taste, then cooked by any other method. Fish are particularly suitable for preserving by smoking; the longer they are left, the drier and harder they become, extending their shelf-life.

COOKING REPTILES

Smaller reptiles such as lizards are best toasted. Snakes and turtles should be cut into small segments and boiled.

COOKING BIRDS AND MAMMALS

These may be cooked whole or in joints. If you are unsure about the tenderness of the flesh, boil it then roast it. Be warned that carnivores taste nasty.

COOKING ROOTS

These are often very tough and require slow baking, roasting or boiling.

COOKING POT HERBS

Always boil these. It may be necessary to boil them in several changes of water to remove undesirable, strong-tasting acids.

COOKING FRUITS

Eat succulent, soft varieties raw, but bake the thick-skinned, tougher types.

▲ Primitive Equipment

It is extremely difficult to manufacture basic tools without a knife or small hatchet, but not impossible. You may be able to fashion simple tools and cooking equipment from wreckage or by adapting the items you are carrying. A metal air-filter housing from some engines makes a good pan, for example. Metal hubcaps can be used as boiling pans, and plastic ones as plates. Stripped wiring can be burned clean of plastic and then used to make wire hangers to hold pans and other items over the fire.

If you can cut a section out of large bamboo, you can use the sealed compartments between segments to boil water or cook food. Knocking the segments through in small bamboo makes a very effective straw, while the very thin varieties can be used as chopsticks. This saves you from burning your fingers, and besides, your hands will be very unhygienic unless you regularly wash with purified water!

In a survival situation you soon realize how much you take for granted; even cooking and eating become major problems.

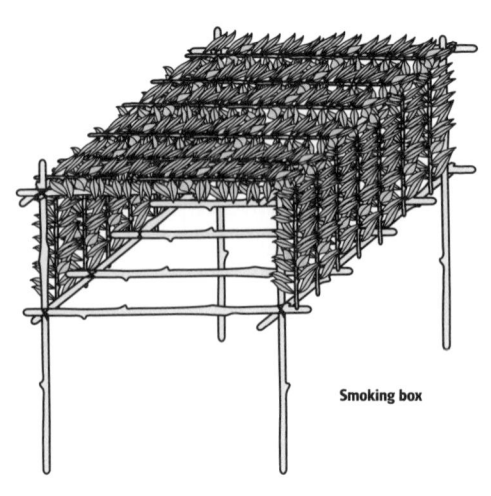

Smoking box

Primitive Equipment

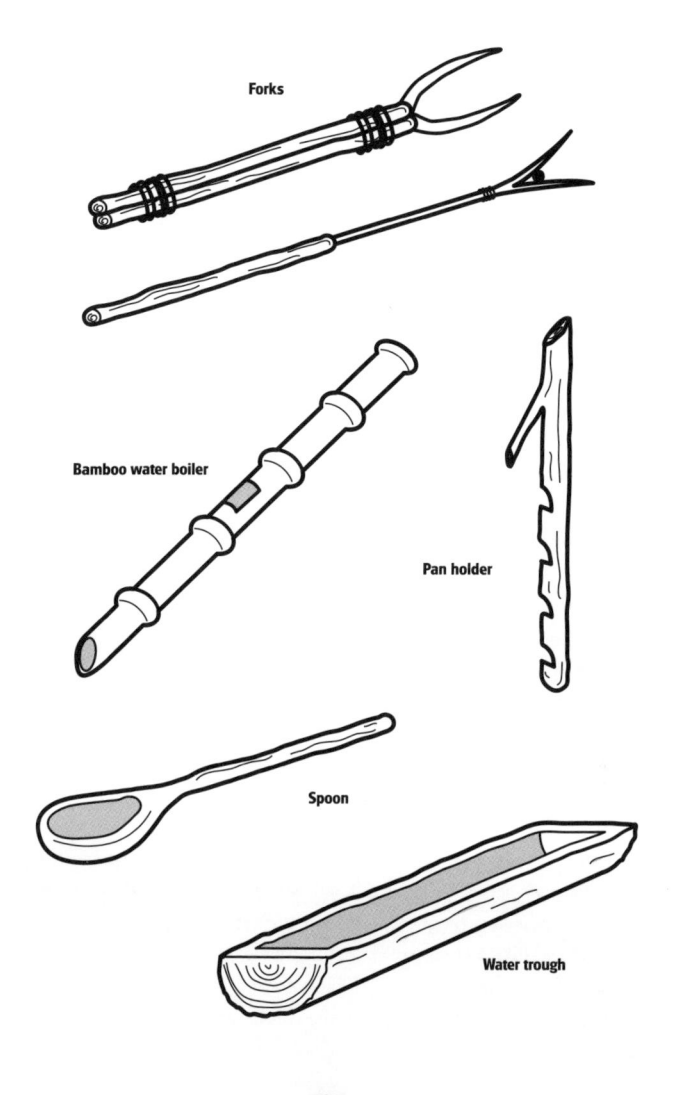

Forks

Bamboo water boiler

Pan holder

Spoon

Water trough

▲ Hunting and Trapping

Before you can eat wild creatures, you first have to catch them – which means hunting or trapping them. Whatever method you use, always kill your prey quickly and efficiently, with minimum distress to the animal.

You may have to stalk your prey – that is, follow and approach it stealthily and silently. It is not easy.

- ▲ **Approach prey with the wind in your face; all wild animals have a keen sense of smell, and even on a calm day, air carries human scent a long way**
- ▲ **If possible, try to keep the sun behind you, especially if low in the sky; animals do not see well when looking into bright sunlight**
- ▲ **In woodland, move very slowly and avoid standing on twigs. Watch for low branches and foliage that may make a noise when brushed. Animals only make noise in woodland when they flee danger, and other animals hear this and hide**
- ▲ **In mountainous areas, noise from falling rocks is common, and a little such noise rarely spooks game**
- ▲ **Approach grazing animals from a higher position; they expect threats from lower down**
- ▲ **In snowy areas, hunt in fresh snow, as footsteps in crisp snow and ice echo for quite a distance**
- ▲ **Keep off game trails; all wild animals constantly watch their back trails**

TRAPPING

Trapping is the most productive way of avoiding starvation. There are few areas with no game to eat; the problem is finding and catching it. You may get lucky with a home-made bow or spear, but will more likely spend a lot of time making and then learning enough accuracy to kill food for a meal. Without outdoor hunting experience, you may well use more energy locating and killing your game than you get from eating it! Trapping does takes time and skill, but once traps are set they are working even when you are asleep. You can always try your hand at hunting once the traps are set; nothing ventured, nothing gained.

Being successful takes practice and patience. With time and experience, you should be able to keep yourself and others supplied with enough food to survive. Trapping involves good preparation, planning and patience. Even with no experience, you can make a simple trap and catch local game. Luck plays a big part in the early stages, as few people know where to find game or how to set traps properly. In time, these skills will become second nature. Early on, it helps if you think about what you are trying to achieve and follow the basic rules.

BASIC RULES OF TRAPPING

Where possible, use streams and other water features to travel to and from your traps. Water does not hold scent and will mask the noise of your approach. Crushed vegetation has a strong smell; if there is a lot of disturbance, animals become wary, and will go around the hazard. If you have no choice, do not go back to the trap; leave it and check it regularly from a distance. The ground re-establishes itself soon enough and the game will use the trail again.

If your shelter is made of wreckage, and/or you use oil and fuel for fire-lighting, keep your trapping equipment, footwear and clothing well away from the shelter area. Even tiny amounts of oil leave a strong scent that lingers for a very long time, and no game will approach.

Where possible, leave your traps at their locations, well away from the campsite. If you have to move them, store them well outside the camp area. If they become contaminated by any human source, decontaminate them by hanging them in the smoke of the camp fire. Animals are used to the smell of smoke, and will return to the hunting area when they realize that there is no fire present.

When you have set your traps, use a very light covering of local vegetation as camouflage. Use material that you can find without disturbing the immediate location. Too much may foul the trap or spring it prematurely. Also, avoid building traps at ground level; game will not climb on to a trap. Well-set trail traps must be dug in slightly below ground level. In winter, frost can freeze the trap-triggers, preventing tripping, so set snares.

GOING FOR THE KILL

A professional trap will kill its prey in a split second, without the creature knowing anything about it. Unfortunately, badly-positioned traps can catch animals by their legs or half-way down their bodies. Not killed outright, the animals pull, turn and twist in their attempts to break free, leaving them badly cut, in pain and terrified. Even experienced trappers have traps that partly fail, catching but not killing the animal.

Hunting and Trapping

Always take great care approaching any trapped animal; even the most unlikely can give you a serious injury. The only safe way is to kill the animal with a heavy, hard pole or iron bar (known as a priest). Hit the creature on the back of the neck with enough force to break it. If you think you have only stunned it, make sure by pushing a sharp knife through the creature's neck behind the windpipe and cutting towards the back of the neck. This will cut through the main arteries and quickly finish the animal.

BIRD TRAPS

One of the simplest ways of trapping large seed-eating birds is to bait a fish-hook with seed or a piece of fruit and secure it to a strong fishing line, making sure the line is tied securely. Throw a few seeds around the area, and a bird will peck at the bait and become caught on the fish-hook.

If you have plenty of line, look for an area where birds roost or there are plenty of nests. Tie lengths of the line to branches to secure them, and then tie running nooses on all the lines. Birds will land on the branches and step into the nooses, getting their feet caught and trapping them.

Spring snares are good for catching large ground-feeding game birds such as pheasants. The spring should be a young sapling with plenty of power. Tie two pieces of twine, cord or heavy fishing line to the sapling and bend it down so that the strings touch the ground. Mark the spot where it touches. Let the sapling return to its original position.

Now carefully dig a hole approximately four inches (10cm) in diameter and six inches (15cm) deep, and knock a securing peg deep into the centre of the hole; secure a second peg to one string leading from the sapling. Tie a snare in the second line. Push the second peg through the snare, pull the sapling down so that the second peg meets the peg in the hole and connect the two pegs together by cutting fairly tight interlocking grooves to form the trigger. Pull the snare out so that it encircles the hole; then spread a little bait around the area, finishing with a plentiful supply of bait in the hole.

The game bird will take the bait from around the hole and eventually put its head in the hole to take the bait. This dislodges the peg trigger, at which point the spring of the sapling will straighten, lifting the snare and catching the bird, breaking its neck as it snatches it off the ground.

WATER-FOWL TRAPS

The stilt duck trap – taught to me by survival expert Eddie McGee – is simple to build and use. In shallow water, take three straight pieces of timber and put them in a tripod-shape below the water line. Attach a simple snare or float and baited fish-hook to a heavy, flat stone, and balance the rock on the tripod. The trap is sprung when the water-fowl swims up to take the bait. Once it has been caught, it will struggle, kick the tripod and dislodge the stone. This sinks, dragging the bird underwater and holding it there until it drowns.

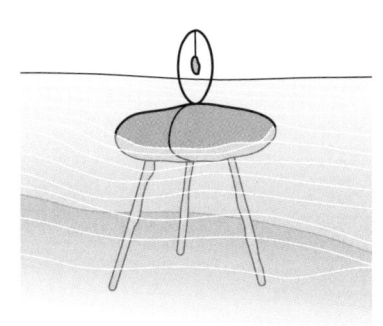

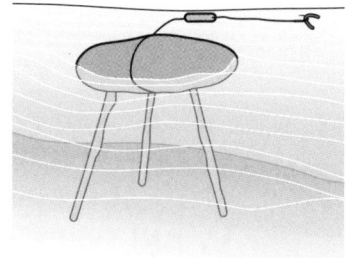

FISH TRAPS

The best-known fish trap is the fishing rod, which is very easy to make and use. Use a fresh, young sapling, two to three metres long, as your rod and a bent wire if you have no sharp hook. Fish will take any bait if it is presented well; strips of silver paper, feathers and scraps of metal slowly pulled across the water can all catch fish. Live bait can be found by digging up worms, or stripping the bark from dead trees and collecting the insects behind.

A simple maze can make a very effective river trap. The poles should be approximately 2.75 inches (7cm) in diameter and hammered into the riverbed one inch (5cm) apart. The trap shepherds fish into the funnel and holds them in the tank. The river easily flows through, but larger fish are caught.

In tidal waters, constructing a wall makes a very effective trap. As the water recedes, a reservoir is created, holding the fish. The wall should be horseshoe-shaped, approximately one metre above the surface at the highest point grading to ground level at each end. The opening should face the land. Tides are strong, so the rocks must be heavy enough not to move. The trap is covered by water at high tide and exposed during low tide, when it should be checked.

Hunting and Trapping

A smaller, quicker fish trap can be made by making two circles out of very flexible thin twigs. The first circle should be 12 inches (30cm) in diameter and the second five inches (13cm). Attach long, slender twigs to the largest circle and tie the ends together to form a cone shape with a bait inside the tip. Push the second circle down into the cone. Attach several twigs facing inwards and down to the cone so that when the fish passes through the second ring to retrieve the bait, the prongs stop it from swimming backwards to escape. Secure the trap on the river bed, with the mouth of the cone facing upstream.

SMALL GAME TRAPS

The snare is the easiest trap to construct and use, and can be very productive. This is basically a noose with the free end tied down firmly. The animal puts its head through the noose, tightening it as it runs and snapping its neck. Snares can be made from many materials – strong string, animal sinew, strips of plaited animal skin, heavy fishing line: anything flexible, supple and strong.

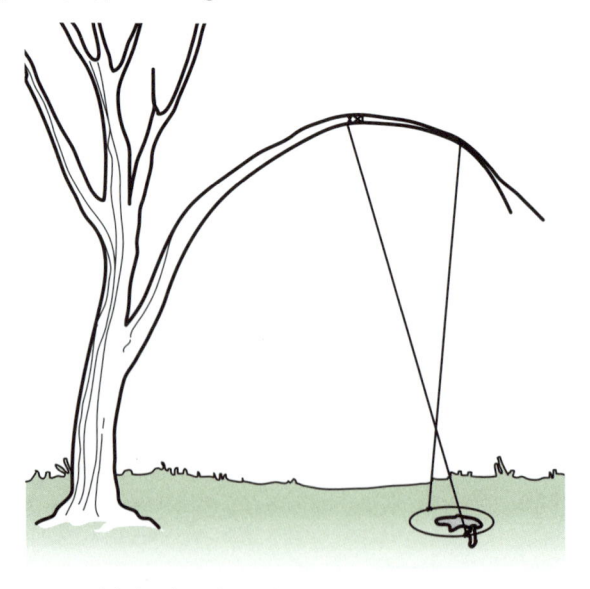

A simple spring trap is a good way to catch ground-feeding birds.

Hunting and Trapping

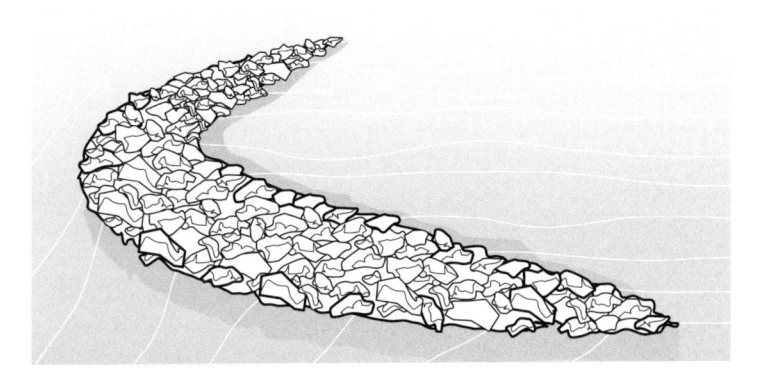

Being able to make simple traps, such as the tidal fish trap above, will ensure that you can catch enough food to aid your survival.

The snare should be firmly secured – saplings and other deep-rooted branched vegetation are ideal – and set along an animal trail. For rabbits, the noose should be approximately five inches (14cm) in diameter and set so that the bottom of the noose is five inches (14cm) from the ground, about the size of an adult fist with the thumb straightened. For hares, the bottom of the noose should be seven inches (19cm) high, approximately an adult hand-span, because hares run head-up.

Hedgehogs are good food and can easily be caught in a bucket trap. Dig a hole 12 inches (30cm) in diameter and 12 inches (30cm) deep, with sides sloping inwards so the animal cannot climb out. Use a little animal fat to bait the trap. The hedgehog will climb in to eat it but be unable to escape.

⚠ What to Eat

All free-running game is safe to eat, as are birds' eggs. Some taste better than others, but taste becomes less of a problem as you become hungrier! Never eat anything you find dead, and avoid animals that makes little effort to avoid capture, as they are probably dying through illness or poison anyway; either way, you do not want to risk the same fate. Once you have killed your prey, leave it to hang for a while to give the body heat time to disperse. Eating meat and fish when it is too fresh can cause an upset stomach.

Seafood is a good source of protein, but tends to deteriorate quickly once exposed to air. Many fish, especially in the tropics, have poison spines and skin, so avoid fish with spines or which are particularly ugly. Other edible seafoods include snails, clams, muscles, limpets, sea urchins, sea cucumber, scallops and starfish.

Most seaweed is safe to eat either raw or cooked, but make sure that you have lots of fresh water, as the body needs it to digest seaweed. Only eat fresh seaweed, which is firm to the touch, smooth and has no offensive odours. Some varieties are very high in irritant acids. Crush a little. If it has high irritant content it will omit an offensive smell within ten minutes. Boil such seaweed in at least two changes of water to remove the acid.

DRESSING FISH

Used your priest to kill the fish. Scrape off scales by holding the fish's tail and scraping with the back of a knife or sharp stone down towards the head. This is best done in water so that the scales wash off as you work. Once they have been removed, hold the fish by its head, belly-up, and insert your knife just below the head; then cut the fish to just before the tail. Cut deep enough to cut through the flesh, but not so deep as to slice the innards. Scrape the cavity clean in water, leaving none of the stomach inside. The head can be removed by cutting behind the gills, and the tail and fins can just be cut away.

DRESSING SMALL BIRDS

Holding the bird firmly in one hand, use the thumb and first finger of your free hand to pluck out a few feathers at a time; if you take too many, you risk ripping the flesh. Leave the neck and head. Once done, cut the neck just above the breast, and cut the legs off by slicing through the joint at the knee. Lie the bird on its back and cut a circle around the anus, just deep enough to cut through the flesh, taking care not to cut into the innards. Pull the flesh down and push your second finger into the cavity and over the top of the innards, keeping the back of your finger close to the breast bone. When it is fully inserted, bend it over the back of the innards and scoop them all out. If possible, wash the bird inside and out, making sure that there are no innards remaining.

DRESSING LARGE BIRDS

Plucking a large bird is best done by placing it on your lap, with its neck and head between your knees, holding its feet together with one hand. From this position you can easily pluck the bird clean. Proceed as per small birds above. Once the anus is cut, you will have to push the whole of your hand inside the cavity to scrape the innards out.

In both of the above cases, save feathers for insulation by plucking the bird over a hole and putting the feathers in. Once they're collected, either keep innards for trap and fish bait or scrape them into the hole and bury them. Heart and liver, if distinguishable, can be safely cooked and eaten.

DRESSING ANIMALS

Hang the dead animal by its rear legs, belly towards you. Use the tip of your knife to cut through the skin only. Do not cut into the flesh. The best way is to pinch a little fur/skin near one of the rear feet and pull it away from the leg. Cut horizontally through the pinch. Then insert the point of your knife from above, with the back of the knife facing in towards the flesh.

Carefully slice the skin down the length of the leg, finishing at the top centre of the body. Carry out the same procedure on the other leg, joining the cuts to form a 'V' shape. From the bottom of the 'V', continue cutting down the centre of the animal, stopping at the head. Use the knife to cut the skin from around the legs. Skin the front legs using the same technique, then cut the skin away from around the stomach. From the rear of the animal, pull the skin down, exposing the body flesh, stopping when it reaches the head. Cut the skin from the body and save it for stretching and drying.

What to Eat

Next, cut the animal open by inserting the point of your knife above the rib cage deep enough to cut the flesh, but not so deep that it cuts the innards. Run the knife up to open the whole stomach; place your hands inside the body cavity and pull out the innards. When you have done this, cut or chop through the centre of the breastbone and pull out the lungs and heart, which will be attached to the windpipe and head. Pull them down and remove the head.

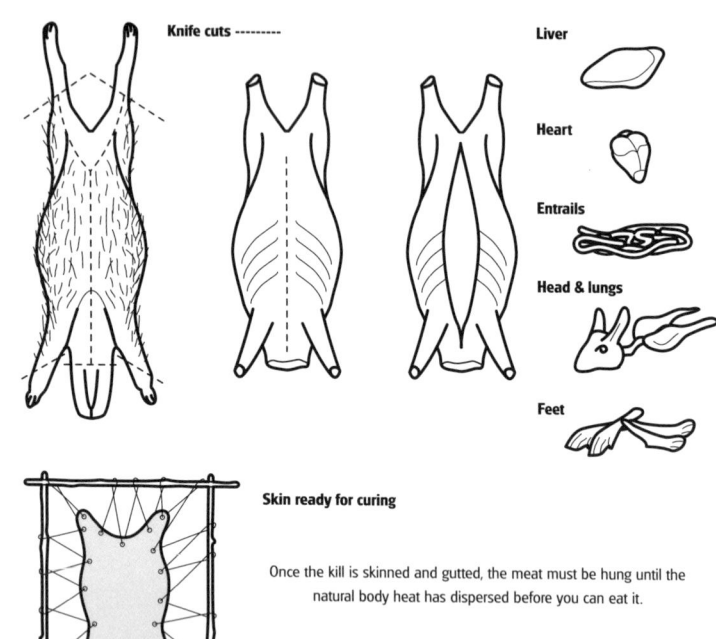

Knife cuts

Liver

Heart

Entrails

Head & lungs

Feet

Skin ready for curing

Once the kill is skinned and gutted, the meat must be hung until the natural body heat has dispersed before you can eat it.

DRESSING RATS

You can find and easily trap rats in most places; using entrails as bait helps. Rats make good eating, but have to be prepared with great care and precision; this is true of all your kills, but even more important with rats. Because they are small, they are difficult to handle. During skinning and gutting, be very careful to ensure no urine is discharged due to poor cutting or killing techniques. Rats carry the disease leptospirosis – commonly known as 'ratcatcher's yellows' – in their urine. It's a very dangerous jaundice-like disease, and you should guard against it at all times. Once the rat is clean, the best ways to cook it are to roast it slowly over hot embers or have it boned, diced and boiled.

SNAILS AND EARTHWORMS

Snails and earthworms are full of protein. Worms can be washed, boiled and eaten straight away, although they are more palatable chopped into small sections and mixed with other food. They're particularly good with eggs.

Snails need a little preparation before they can be consumed. The meat is fine to eat, but snails can eat plant life that is poisonous to humans, so their intestines and stomach need to be cleared of any poisons first. The most effective way of doing this is keeping them in a container and feeding them with fresh vegetation that is safe for humans. If you have any mint available, such as spearmint (Mentha spicata), a little added to their diet will give the snails a good, clean taste. Keep them for two or three days before cooking them whole in a pan of boiling water.

CANNIBALISM

There are several well-documented instances where survivors have had to eat human flesh to avoid starvation. In exceptional survival circumstances, cannibalism does not carry a criminal penalty. Killing another human for food is still murder, however; you can only eat the already dead, and should not risk eating diseased corpses. Whether or not you could bring yourself to cannibalise someone is clearly a matter only you can decide at the time. Living with it afterwards is often very difficult; some people can never recover, despite all the available counselling. Would you want your friends or colleagues to survive by eating your flesh if you were the dead person?

If you do need to cannibalise a human, the carcass has to be dealt with in exactly the same way as any other game. Make sure not to consume any brain matter or spinal tissue, as it can carry fatal diseases.

POISONOUS ANIMALS

The meat of all free-running game is safe to eat. Note, however, that eating too much rabbit and nothing else induces a vitamin deficiency that can cause death. Polar bear and seal liver is also poisonous at certain times of the year.

⚠ Edible/Medicinal Plants

Many plants are nutritious, but it can be tough to spot the poisonous ones. You need to be extra-careful before eating something that you do not recognize. In general, do not eat any plant with a milky sap. Brightly-coloured fruits, especially red ones, should be avoided, as many are full of poisons, and unless you know exactly what you are doing, stay away from mushrooms and other fungi.

GREAT PLANTAIN *(Plantago Major)*

This perennial herb makes a great tonic boiled tea. Drink an eggcupful three times a day against boils. Steeped overnight in cold water, the juice is a cough remedy. The leaves can be warmed and wrapped around aching limbs.

ROSEBAY WILLOW HERB *(Chamaenerion angustifolium)*

Also known as fireweed, the young leaves can be used in salads, and the roots can be use as a tasty vegetable. The younger the plant, the better.

STINGING NETTLE *(Urtica dioica)*

Stinging nettles are excellent for making rope and fine string. The leaves look and taste like spinach. Picking them isn't too bad if you have a pair of gloves. Leather is best; wool is useless. All the leaves can be eaten, but tender young ones are sweeter. Once picked, boil in water for 15 minutes to remove the acid, then drain, put in fresh water and bring back to the boil. You can eat the leaves as they are, add them to stews or fry them with a little animal fat.

Medicinally, thick soup made with the youngest leaves is good for purifying the blood. Nettle stings can locally reduce rheumatism, and personally I can say that on one occasion I got covered in stings after a period of very hard exercise. Once the initial pain wore off, I did not have any of the normal aches I expected.

HAWTHORN *(Rosaceae crataegus monogyna)*

As well as the leaves, the bright red haws can be eaten raw, or cooked and used in salads and stews. Although they have no distinct taste, they do make excellent jam and preserves.

Medicinally, hawthorn is a cardiac sedative. It dilates blood vessels, thereby reducing blood pressure; soak two handfuls of the dried flowers and fresh or dried haws in a little water overnight. Add two teaspoonfuls of the tincture to a cup of water and let stand for 15 minutes. Take the resulting medicine two to four times a day for several weeks, by when it will be working properly. Compote made by adding the fruit to syrup made from the flesh of haws mixed with honey can be given for diarrhoea. The wood has a hard brown heart, and is strong enough to be used to make tools and trap-triggers.

Surviving a Hitchhike

Hitchhiking paints a big target over you that every weirdo on the roads can aim at. That's not to say that you shouldn't do it, but do understand the dangers and be aware of some of the ways to protect yourself. Male or female, do not travel alone; having a travelling partner reduces the risk of becoming a victim. Be under no illusion; attackers come in all shapes, sizes, creeds, colours, mannerisms and genders. Even with a partner, think twice before taking a lift in a vehicle with more than one young male in it.

Plan well before you go. Learn a little about the customs and practices of the countries you are passing through. Circumnavigate unfriendly parts of the world and war zones. Always dress down for the journey in local-neutral clothes. Exposing flesh is dangerous, and illegal in many countries. Likewise, wearing a sports shirt or any other clear home-nation identifier will attract every political, religious and xenophobic extremist for miles.

SURVIVING IN CITIES AND TOWNS

Always be vigilant and pay attention to avoid becoming a victim. Carrying luggage marks you as a traveller and a target for theft. Pickpockets are the likely first wave; distribute money, valuables and official paperwork around your body so you don't lose everything at once. Keep any pocket buttons fastened. Never put a wallet or purse in your back trouser pocket; it is too easy to see. Keep jackets and coats fastened tightly. Take off any jewellery and stow it away until your destination.

CARRYING LUGGAGE

If your luggage, purse or handbag has straps, use them. Keep all your baggage with you all the time, and if you have to put it down either stand astride it or sit on it, with your foot through the straps. If luggage has external pockets, don't put valuables in them. Keep your baggage in front of you.

Modern criminals mostly work in groups, so some can try to put themselves between you and your luggage – or distract you, perhaps physically – while others take your stuff and pass it rapidly from person to person.

Be extra-vigilant in crowds, always avoid groups of young men and remember children can make enthusiastic, skilled and shameless pick-pockets. The worst thing you can do is to open your purse and hand out cash; sadly, you'll trigger a surge of beggars, urchins and thieves. Most child beggars are being forced to work for an abusive parent or 'guardian' anyway; any money you give them will be taken away immediately.

SURVIVING MUGGINGS AND ARMED ASSAULT

Keep as calm as possible and hand over whatever the assailants want, quickly and politely. Goods can be replaced. Your life cannot.

▲ Travelling by Car

Make sure your vehicle has been checked and serviced; there is no excuse for not doing so. All vehicles break down eventually – usually when least expected – so membership of a recognized breakdown service is crucial. While awaiting assistance, keep doors and windows locked. If you have broken down on a motorway, leave the vehicle and stand off the hard shoulder. Many people die each year in hard shoulder accidents. Lone females should keep a pair of loose workman's overalls in the boot, along with a hard-hat or baseball cap, and put these on; tuck any long hair under the cap and passers-by will assume you are male, greatly lessening the risk of dangerous attention.

SURVIVING CAR-JACKING

You can be lulled into a false sense of security driving a car. However, always drive with all doors locked to prevent attack and theft. You'll be surprised how often a car has to stop while driving. If you are conscious after an accident, you can easily unlock a door, and if not, emergency services know how to smash a window.

A favourite carjacking method is to simply wait near a filling station. If keys are left in the vehicle while the driver goes to pay, the car is stolen in moments. Always lock your vehicle every time you leave it, regardless of duration. Another technique is to follow a vehicle and stage a minor accident by bumping into the rear of the target at a quiet road junction. When the driver gets out to view the damage, the hijackers steal the vehicle. Monitor the traffic following you. If a vehicle with two or more occupants has been behind you for some time, be cautious. Pull over to let them past. If they do stop too – rare, even for criminals – then head off again as soon as anyone gets out, and make a bee-line for a police station or busy road or town.

If you are involved in a suspicious minor accident, stay in the vehicle with the doors locked and windows shut. Let the responsible party come to you. Insurance details can be shouted. Do not open the window even a little – they are quite easy to force down – and keep your

Travelling by Car

engine running. Drive away the instant the situation becomes threatening, head to the nearest police station and report the incident. This alerts the police, but you may also need to prove that you were not trying to wilfully flee the scene of an accident.

SURVIVING IN-CAR THEFT

Whenever you are in your vehicle, ensure all valuables are out of sight. Thieves will open your passenger door, reach through an open window or even smash a window in order to grab mobile telephones, wallets, purses, laptop computers or other valuables. Crossroads, busy traffic lights and regular traffic jams are particularly risky. Keeping everything out of sight removes both target and threat.

If someone does enter the car through a window or open door, and you fear for your safety, use an ice-scraper to jab into their hand or face to force them out, or spray de-icer into their eyes. Be very ready to speed off as soon as the attacker has pulled back, however.

EVASIVE DRIVING

If you think you are being followed, adopt evasive driving techniques. For the most part, your ability to escape is determined by the vehicles involved. However, you should drive in the middle of the road, with a slight bias towards your proper lane; a tail will have to pull on to the wrong side of the road for the driver to see if it is safe to pass. If there are oncoming vehicles, the pursuing driver will continually be forced back behind you, and you are already blocking him from passing on the inside.

Where you have a clear view of safety, cut bends to as straight a line as possible. This helps you to keep speed and stops the pursuing vehicle from trying to force you off the road. Keep your car in lower gears as much as possible, as this increase engine control and acceleration.

Have both hands on the wheel, and do not wrap your thumbs inside it; if your front wheels hit an object at speed, the sudden jerk can dislocate your thumbs. Keep braking to a minimum and avoid sharp braking; use gears to slow down. Smoothly operating the accelerator controls speed without losing grip. If you have never carried out an evasive handbrake turn, the middle of a pursuit is not the time to experiment.

SURVIVING THE FLAT TYRE SCAM

Many cars have their spare wheel in the boot – where you also lock your luggage, shopping and valuables. Some organized gangs target parked hire vehicles or cars with out-of-area

Travelling by Car

registration plates, then let one of the tyres down. The occupants will be forced to stop in order to change the wheel, and to get to it, everything has to be taken out. The gang can then snatch the goods. In some cases, the gang may follow the target vehicle, then pull over, pretending to offer help.

If you own a vehicle with a spare wheel in the boot, consider leaving it on top of your luggage so you don't have to unload to get to it. With hire vehicles, ask for a vehicle with the spare stored in a carrier outside. The other alternative is to call roadside assistance to change the wheel for you.

SURVIVING TAXIS

Avoid using taxis and other commercial transport that is not officially licensed. Official taxis usually have at least some checks that the driver is law-abiding and can drive. Don't become too complacent in this, though. It's not difficult to get a job as an official cabbie even with a bad criminal record. As always, if you feel in the least bit uneasy, refuse to get in.

SURVIVING TRAINS

Sitting in the first carriage following the engine, in easy reach of the alarm, should be your preferred position on risky trains – both above-ground and underground. This is particularly true at night or in isolated or lawless areas. It's bad enough waiting around in deserted stations for the train in the first place, without putting yourself at greater risk sitting in a deserted carriage far from the driver.

If you cannot avoid travelling alone, try to journey at times when the trains and stations are busy. In some countries, it is common for passengers to cook food during journeys on little gas burners; the fire risk of these is incredible, so always sit as near the front as possible, as flames will spread faster towards the rear.

Where trains are properly supervised and there is no risk of fire, you are marginally safer in the last carriage; in the event of a crash, you stand a better chance of survival, as most crashes are at the front. Similarly, sitting with your back to the engine may induce mild travel sickness but means any front impact will force you back in your seat rather than throwing you down the carriage. Ideally, sit facing an empty seat to avoid being struck by a flying fellow-passenger.

⚠ Travelling by Air and Sea

Both in the air and at sea, you turn safety and control over to the crew. There is little you can do to maximise safety other than observe the emergency procedures as explained by the crew. Also, take the time to read any emergency information that is supplied.

SURVIVING AIR TRAVEL

On aircraft, your hand luggage may be your only opportunity to stack the odds in your favour. A simple survival kit should include the following items:

- **Waterproofed non-safety matches and plastic-sealed striker strip**
- **A small candle – the night-light type is ideal**
- **A big ball of cotton wool for tinder**
- **Plenty of fishing line**
- **A snare**
- **Water purifying tablets**
- **Condoms (to use as a water carrier)**
- **Pencil and paper**

If the airline allows it – and most will not – then also take a small knife or scalpel, and a couple of packets of fishing hooks. If not, these can still go in hold luggage, and may turn up providentially.

Emergencies and alcohol do not mix. Even one drink can impair your judgement, and you really don't want to be intoxicated in an emergency. Drinking water is a much safer option, and you'll feel fresher at your destination too. If a fellow-passenger is drinking heavily, keep an eye on their location. If you need to act quickly, you don't want to be held up by a drunk.

When you are stuck in one position for many hours, your muscles stiffen. Walk the length of the plane regularly or, if not possible, use simple seated exercises to keep blood flowing. This will not only keep you alert, it also helps stop deep vein thrombosis (DVT).

Be on your guard in airports and on aircraft. Keep a discreet eye open for people acting suspiciously or who are agitated, for suspicious packages and for vehicles parked in restricted

Travelling by Air and Sea

areas. Whenever you feel uncomfortable, bring it to the attention of security staff. Do not fret about reporting something innocent.

If a violent drunk or terrorist must be tackled on an aeroplane, leave this to people near the target. Too many people will trip each other up, allowing the target room to manoeuvre and operate any equipment or weapons. If you are the close one, grab the person in a bear hug, or use a strangle-hold.

SURVIVING SEA TRAVEL

As with aircraft, you should take note of the emergency procedures as demonstrated by the crew. If you have a cabin, you must make sure that you can find the quickest way to the deck, and can remember the route without having to stop and think about it. You will be allocated an emergency muster point, which you should remember and make your way to several times during the voyage. By doing this, you will not only remember the most efficient route to take, but can monitor any changes or obstacles that may have appeared since your first visit.

In your cabin, make sure that you keep warm, protective clothing by your door so that you can grab it in an emergency. Even in hot climates, if you have to evacuate the ship you will find that a lifeboat at sea can be both cold and wet. What you do not want is to be woken in the middle of the night and have to leave your cabin immediately without adequate clothing; staying behind after the emergency signal and searching your luggage for outdoor clothes will lessen your chances of survival. It will help you if you keep a small store of simple, non-perishable food such as boiled sweets in your emergency clothing pockets. A small survival kit, such as the one mentioned in the aircraft section above, should also be kept with your clothing. Survival is about proper preparation. Prepare well in advance, and you will have the best chance of living through the ordeal.

SURVIVING A SHIPWRECK

Once you have evacuated the ship and have taken to a lifeboat, you should pay attention to the vessel's senior member, who will be an experienced member of the ship's crew. If there is not a member of the ship's company aboard, there will be an instruction booklet, along with fresh water and emergency rations stowed in the boat. As soon as you board the lifeboat, make every effort to steer it away from the ship. Once you are a safe distance away, have your emergency signal equipment ready for immediate use, and attend to any injuries that you or your fellow survivors may have. Having completed this task, take the time to read the emergency booklet and plan your future action.

Unless you are absolutely sure that no international emergency signal has been sent, stay in the area of the wreckage; the ship's radio operator will have signalled the position to the rescuers, and there will also be automatically-operated equipment that sends out radio distress signals when in contact with seawater. If there are other lifeboats in the area, join together with them to make as large a platform as possible. This will ensure that you can share the experience of others, help to protect everyone from capsizing and help the rescuers to see you; all you have to do then is wait until the rescuers reach you.

If you have moved away from the site, head for land. If you are unsure, look for clouds building in an otherwise clear sky, as clouds build over land. If there is bird life you are probably relatively close to land. Early in the morning birds will fly away from land, whereas late in the afternoon and evening they will be returning to it.

SURVIVING AVALANCHES

Avalanches are unpredictable, but should always be expected in snow-covered mountain areas. There are several ways in which an avalanche can occur. Loud noises are a major cause, and this is particularly dangerous when search-and-rescue aircraft are flying in the vicinity. Falling rocks or high winds can also start the movement of large areas of unstable snow and ice. Snow becomes very unstable when there is a quick thaw. After a heavy snowfall, the loose, new snow builds a deep layer on top of old, compacted snow. This can then be disturbed and it will slide away, cascading down the mountain.

If you are travelling in areas that are prone to avalanches, be aware of thawing conditions, high winds, sudden heavy snowfalls and rain. If you have to travel in these conditions, keep away from steep faces, gullies and overhanging snow masses.

If, however, you are unfortunate enough to get caught in an avalanche, quickly discard any equipment such as skis, snowshoes or luggage you are carrying, as these will hamper your movements. If you can, move to the outer edges of the avalanche, where the force will be relatively less. When you are hit by the wall of snow, force yourself on top of it – rather like surfing a wave – and lie as flat as you can and try to stay on top. Using swimming strokes will help you to do this. As the avalanche comes to a halt, cover your nose and mouth by cupping your hands; doing this will create an air space. When the avalanche fully stops, use your hands to dig as large a space as possible around you before the snow freezes. If you can't get out, keep still in order to conserve your energy and oxygen until help arrives.

SURVIVING VOLCANOES

Volcanic eruptions are generally predictable. However, there are occasions when one erupts without warning or is in such a location that the local population have nowhere to go to escape it. You may well be caught up in either of these situations, and will have to do the best you can to survive.

Where a volcano erupts with force, a large quantity of very hot lava may be thrown out of it. If you are within the area of its fallout, you should get under cover; this may be in the cellars of buildings, under rock overhangs or any other place that protects you from falling hazards. Avoid getting under vehicles, as these may well catch fire and explode. Cover your mouth and nose with a damp scarf or handkerchief, and breathe through your nose to cut down on the inhalation of gases and dust.

After the initial eruption, the volcano will probably continue to spew molten rock that will create a lava flow. This rarely moves at a great speed, but can still move sufficiently quickly to catch people out. To avoid getting caught up in it and the inevitable fires it causes, keep moving steadily away from the flow.

Even after the flow has come to a halt and the lava solidifies, do not climb on or over it, as the inner lava takes a long time to cool properly. The surface may look and feel hard enough to walk on, but you can fall through and be horribly burnt. Likewise, there is still a danger of poisonous gases for some considerable time after the initial blow.

⚠ Escape and Evasion

Never underestimate either life or people. Both will take you by surprise regularly. Although it may seem unlikely that you would ever need to use escape and evasion skills to survive, you never know. As a part of your overall survival, you may well need to evade a pursuer or escape from detention, and you might need evasion skills until you can reach a safe place or meet up with people who can help you.

Having effected an escape, the last thing you want is to be captured again. Once you have cleared the immediate vicinity, choose an area that gives you good cover. Keep moving for as long as you can, watching your back trail as well as your forward route. Moving around creates noise, so you should take care to move deliberately, and avoid fast, jerky movements, which will draw attention to your position; easy, flowing movements are not so easily seen.

If your route takes you through dense undergrowth or some other area where the human form is alien, you must break up your body shape and facial features; using camouflage made from vegetation and other material in the locality will help you to stay hidden. Tying local vegetation to your clothing and applying crushed berries and mud on your face and hands does not take long, and will create good camouflage.

EVASIVE MOVEMENT

Hiding by day and moving by night may well help you to evade capture, but moving in unfamiliar territory in the dark is not an easy option. When you are moving, keep off local paths, roads and highways, as these will be in constant use. If you have to cross open ground, keep to the edges; do not walk in the open or across crop fields, deserts or snow even at night, as your tracks can easily be seen from the air.

When possible, walk near flowing water; using the noise this type of feature makes may give you the opportunity to move very quickly without being heard. Do not walk on exposed ridges or over the tops of hills, as you will easily be seen against the sky. Change your course as often as possible, and climb through rock falls and over hard ground to mask your tracks.

Keep away from local dwellings, as these may contain dogs that can hear you and alert the residents with their barking.

If you think dogs may be tracking you, walk in streams or through fields that contain livestock such as cattle. Be prepared for a dog attack; carry a stout, short log to use as a cosh in your stronger hand, and wrap spare clothing around your weaker forearm. If a dog does attack, offer it the protected forearm and, once the dog has grasped it, hit the dog at the back of the neck with the club; this blow should be made with sufficient force to break the dog's neck and kill it.

First Aid

We should all have some knowledge of basic first aid, as it is useful not only in a survival situation, but also in our everyday lives. The following information is included in order to give you a taste of the essentials, but I strongly recommend that you attend one of the many courses set up to teach the subject professionally.

In the first instance, you will have to decide which of the injured require the most attention: a difficult decision as, in a plane crash, for example, the injuries are going to be many and horrific. The rule of thumb used by emergency personnel is that someone who is strong enough to scream is a lower priority than someone too weak to make noise.

In all situations, your priorities as a first aider are, in order:
- Keep the casualty alive.
- Stop the harmful condition from getting worse.
- Aid eventual recovery.
- Relieve suffering.

FIRST AID KITS

Outdoor activity and travel shops stock a wide range of first aid kits especially suitable for the traveller. The type and size you need depend on the extent of your travel, the type of activities you are planning to undertake, your carrying capacity and the number of people involved. To these you can add medicines specific to your geographical location, and any personal medication.

Kits can be heavy and bulky, so bear this in mind when purchasing or assembling your own. On small expeditions, individual medical kits that include personal medication are better than a single, communal one. When you are carrying personal medication, make sure that the other members of the group know what it is and how to administer it, as well as any possible side-effects.

Always check that your kit is serviceable before departure; medicines go out of date. I myself once hurt a colleague with a muscle-pain relief cream that caused nasty blistering because it was old.

First aid kit

The golden rule when choosing your kit is to keep it simple. On all my trips, no matter how small, I carry the following:

- Several large squares of lint
- Bandages in various widths
- Sticking plasters (moleskin for blisters)
- Several extra-large plasters
- A roll of surgical tape
- Cotton wool
- Safety pins (not always hand-baggage-friendly anymore)
- Tube of antiseptic cream
- Bicarbonate of soda
- Scissors (not in hand baggage)

ACCIDENT PROCEDURE

After the initial shock of the accident wears off, you need to be able to follow a set routine. This minimizes the risk of poor decision-making, and allows you to carry on quickly with the job in hand. The recognized procedure is:

- ▲ **Carry out immediate first aid.**
- ▲ **Never leave any injured or exhausted person alone.**
- ▲ **Keep casualties warm and comfortable.**
- ▲ **Regularly reassure the patient and other members of the group.**

MOUTH TO MOUTH

Someone who is not breathing needs immediate attention. Once you are satisfied that a person has actually stopped breathing, carry out the following procedure immediately; any time lost will result in permanent brain damage due to the lack of oxygen to this vital organ:

- ▲ **Place the casualty on his back, insulating him from the ground. Check the mouth, nose and throat, and clear if necessary. If the throat is blocked, roll the patient on his side and give a sharp slap between the shoulder blades. If this is impracticable because of his position or contra-indications, use the index finger to clear the obstruction.**
- ▲ **Approaching the casualty from the side, pull up the lower jaw, holding your free hand under the patient's neck so that the head is tilting back and the neck is stretched to allow the free passage of air to the lungs. Check that the tongue is not blocking the airway.**

First Aid

While holding the back of the neck as described, pinch the patient's nostrils shut with the thumb and forefinger of your other hand, then remove the hand supporting the neck and pull the lower jaw open, making sure that the neck remains uppermost and stretched.

Seal the casualty's mouth with yours, and blow air into the mouth approximately every four seconds. You may feel more comfortable using a piece of open woven cloth, such as your handkerchief, between you and the patient. Release the seal on the mouth and turn your head to the side when taking fresh air, as this stops you inhaling the carbon dioxide being exhaled by the patient. It is most important that you take a normal breath, as constantly taking large amounts of air may hyperventilate you. Continue this procedure until the patient's chest rises spontaneously and there is the sound of air leaving the mouth. Allow the casualty to resume breathing unaided.

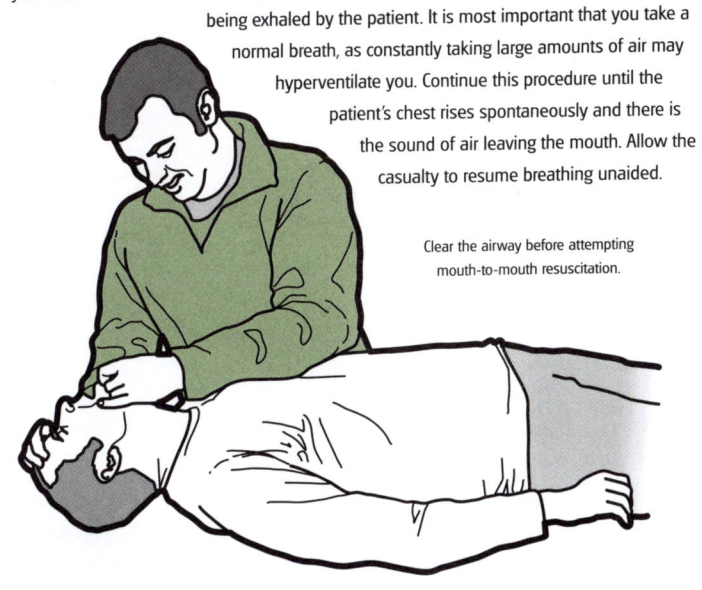

Clear the airway before attempting mouth-to-mouth resuscitation.

- ▲ **Continue to check that the tongue is not blocking the airway.**
- ▲ **The throat may become blocked during this procedure, with vomit or blood stopping the air from reaching the lungs. Slapping the patient between the shoulder blades as before should clear this. Wipe the mouth, clear the throat and resume blowing.**
- ▲ **Keep the casualty warm, and after he has revived treat him as a stretcher case no matter how well he feels. He should be placed in the recovery position.**

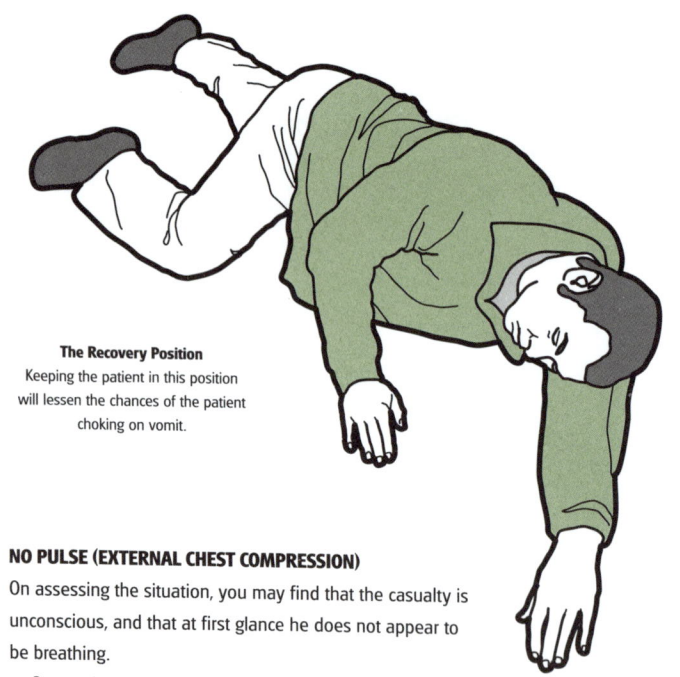

First Aid

The Recovery Position
Keeping the patient in this position will lessen the chances of the patient choking on vomit.

NO PULSE (EXTERNAL CHEST COMPRESSION)

On assessing the situation, you may find that the casualty is unconscious, and that at first glance he does not appear to be breathing.

Stop and consider the cause. Check the heartbeat by taking the pulse; if no pulse is present, then the heart has stopped beating and immediate action is required. It is important that you keep the blood circulating around the body to supply the vital organs. This can be done by external cardiac massage as detailed below.

Place the casualty on their back on a flat, hard surface. Locate the lower part of the breastbone (the bony part of the centre of the chest, just above the stomach); place the heel of your hand over the bone and the heel of your other hand over the first; interlock the fingers, making sure the palms and fingers are well clear of the patient's chest – only the heel of the hand should be in contact with the body.

Keeping your arms straight and locked at the elbows, rock forward, firmly pressing down on the chest bone; you should repeat this pumping action approximately every second. Keep the pressure steady and controlled, avoiding sudden jerking. This procedure pumps blood around the body to the vital organs. However, blood alone will not be sufficient, as it needs to be oxygenated.

This involves mouth-to-mouth breathing as already described. You should combine the two procedures in the following way:

- **Give five chest compressions.**
- **Follow that by one breath.**
- **Repeat until the casualty revives, or professional help arrives.**

REMEMBER
- Place the heel of the hand over the lower part of the breastbone.
- Place the heel of the other hand over the first (keep palms and fingers off the body).
- Rock forwards (straight arms) five times.
- Give one mouth-to-mouth breath.
- Repeat the above steps for as long as you can.
- When breathing and heartbeat are both present, check for spinal injury; if none is present, put the patient in the recovery position.

No matter how good the recovery is, treat the patient as a stretcher case and evacuate him to hospital as soon as the situation allows. Keep checking that the casualty is not vomiting; if so, keep the airway clear.

UNCONSCIOUSNESS
This condition covers everything from a faint to a complete coma. Causes of unconsciousness can include lack of food, low blood pressure, loss of blood, a blow to the head and severe injury. You should view all cases with concern; always put the casualty in the recovery position, and check for breathing and pulse.

Treating the unconscious

Do not: Place a pillow under the head.
Do: Send for help.
   Loosen clothing, especially around the waist and neck.
   Check that the airway is clear – vomit kills.

First Aid

Remember to keep the casualty in the recovery position, which allows the vomit to spew out and keeps the patient from inhaling it; an unconscious patient may be unable to swallow or gag properly

BLEEDING

Do not use a tourniquet! More men lost limbs from the misuse of tourniquets during the First World War than from any type of war wound. A tourniquet restricts the flow of blood to tissue, which causes the tissue to die, resulting in gangrene which, in turn, results in the eventual amputation of the limb if you are lucky, and death if you are not!

Heavy pressure directly over the wound will stop 99% of bleeding. If blood is spurting out, apply thumb or finger pressure down into the wound and keep it there.

SHOCK

This condition is defined as a state of prostration that is found in injured or traumatised persons. There is some degree of shock in all cases of injury – no matter how slight. The symptoms to look for are listed below, but they will not all be present. However, any two should be enough for you to act.

- **Shallow, irregular breathing**
- **Weak, rapid pulse**
- **Cold and clammy skin**
- **Extreme pallor usually, but in some cases the skin appears bluish or even flushed**
- **Dilated pupils (unusually large)**
- **Thirst**
- **Nausea**
- **Weakness, fainting, dizziness**
- **Lack of awareness or even unconsciousness**

You must:

- Keep the patient warm and comfortable, but avoid overheating.
- Give warm, sweet drinks – unless the patient has injuries that would require hospitalization.
- Relieve pain by giving analgesics, but not if the patient is unconscious or showing contra-indications, such as internal bleeding or a head injury.
- Give regular reassurance throughout the recovery.
- Keep the patient's feet slightly higher than his head.

EXPOSURE AND EXHAUSTION

Exposure is severe chilling of the body surface, causing a progressive fall of body temperature with the risk of death from hypothermia-deficient body heat.

Physical exhaustion is an additional risk factor over and above the deficiency of body heat that kills quickly. You must be constantly on the look-out for exhaustion in your group. In the majority of exposure-related fatalities, it has been impossible to separate the effects of one from the other.

It is very difficult to determine the early stages of mild exposure and exhaustion. You must constantly be on the look-out for any of the following signs:

▲ **Complaints of feeling cold, tired or listless**
▲ **Unexpected or unreasonable behaviour**
▲ **Sudden, uncontrollable shivering**
▲ **Physical or mental lethargy, which includes a failure to understand or respond to questions or orders**
▲ **Slowing down or stumbling**
▲ **Disturbed or failed vision**
▲ **Violent outbursts of energy or speech**
▲ **Slurring speech**
▲ **Collapse, stupor or unconsciousness.**

AGGRAVATING EXPOSURE

The following factors will aggravate exposure, and must be eliminated before recovery can take place:

- ▲ **Soaked clothing, especially with high winds**
- ▲ **General chilling from low air temperatures**
- ▲ **Immersion in water, which quickly drains body heat**
- ▲ **Immobility due to injury, which reduces the patient's ability to generate heat**
- ▲ **The combination of fatigue, anxiety, cold and mental stress – this is particularly dangerous**
- ▲ **Unusual thinness**
- ▲ **Alcoholic beverages.**

Alcohol in particular flushes blood to the skin, so you feel warm whilst suffering acute exposure. On a winter training exercise in Norway, I shared a snow-hole with a young heavy drinker. While I was away one night, he drank the better part of a bottle of rum that he had smuggled past me. I returned to find him sprawled out over his sleeping bag with nothing more than a pair of underpants between him and the sub-zero temperature.

On the floor was his empty rum bottle, and in his hand was a half-eaten can of frozen beans and sausages; in his drunken stupidity, he had not bothered to cook the meal but had begun eating it frozen from the can. His body was beginning to turn waxy white and his lips were a bluish grey; another five or ten minutes and he would never have been revived. He was lucky that the weather was clear enough for a helicopter evacuation, and that the field hospital was used to dealing with hypothermia.

The elements are potentially lethal; give them the respect they deserve, and be wary of drinking heavily any time you need to go out in the cold. Many die that way each year.

COLD-WEATHER PROTOCOL

A thorough knowledge of the symptoms, first aid and an understanding of wind chill will all help, but above all prevention is better than cure. The 'Buddy Buddy' system is the safest solution, where men are paired off to watch over each other at all times. By adopting this method, the early symptoms of exposure and exhaustion can be recognized and action taken before reaching the stage at which injury and death occur.

> ## Memory aid
>
> Another good military aid is the mnemonic 'cold feet': a memory-aid checklist for safety in the cold.
>
> C - Clean clothing.
> O - Overheating is out.
> L - Loose layers only.
> D - Dryness demanded.
>
> F - Face, finger, and toe exercises.
> E - Equipment checked and serviceable.
> E - Eat your rations.
> T - Tight boots are terrible.

In an emergency, your procedure should be as follows:

- Prevent further heat loss. Put the casualty into a sleeping, plastic, bivvy or survival bag, ensuring that he is well insulated from the ground and from the sides, including head and face (a balaclava is ideal).
- Get his buddy into the bag with him to supply body heat.
- Protect both of them from the elements.
- Get the rest of the party working to erect a shelter over them or construct a windbreak. This also helps the remainder of the party to keep warm.
- Watch the casualty to check that their breathing or pulse does not stop. In either case, resuscitation and/or external cardiac massage must be started immediately.
- As soon as possible, brew a hot drink, ensuring everyone in the party has something warm to drink and something to eat.
- In all cases of accident or emergency you should send for help, but before the messengers are sent out make sure that they have rested, had a drink, are not suffering from exhaustion and are capable of safely carrying out the task. You must not put others at risk.
- The casualty must be treated as a stretcher-case no matter how well he recovers.

FROSTBITE

Frostbite occurs when the body tissue freezes: this is when a skin temperature of -1°C is reached. The timescale depends on the severity of the cold air, wind speed, the area of flesh exposed and the amount of blood constriction.

First Aid

Minor frostbite mostly affects the body's extremities, such as the nose, cheeks, ears and fingers. This is partly due to the difficulty of insulating these areas sufficiently, but also because of the body's defence mechanism. As the body becomes colder, the blood supply restricts itself to the body core in an effort to preserve inner body heat. Severe frostbite occurs mainly in the feet; the location and shape of the feet make it particularly difficult to insulate them against heat loss, and tight footwear is another contributory factor.

There is a well-proven procedure to prevent frostbitten feet. Simply remove footwear and socks and massage the feet for 10–15 minutes (do not rub them, as your skin will be extremely fragile at this stage). Do this often, and you will not get frostbite. Always keep a spare pair of dry socks next to your skin (I usually keep mine around my stomach) to change into, and change your socks at least once daily. When you bed down, remove your footwear and massage your feet. Avoid sleeping with your footwear on, but if you have no alternative, make sure the laces are undone and the footwear is slack-fitting.

FROSTBITE RECOVERY

Should you suffer from frostbite, then the following action should aid recovery:

- ▲ The affected parts will become painful: this should be sufficient warning, and you should warm them immediately. At this stage, cover the affected parts and get into some form of shelter. Use the 'Buddy Buddy' system; place feet, ears and nose against your mate's skin. If these symptoms occur when you are alone, use the naturally warmer parts of your own body to warm them. In both cases, keep the rest of the body well insulated from the cold. Once the pain ceases and normal sensations return, the danger is over.

- ▲ Some people may be so preoccupied or stunned with cold and exhaustion that they do not notice pain. Eventually it subsides as the area becomes numb. When this occurs, the affected area takes on a waxy white appearance and becomes hard to the touch. This stage is serious, and action must be taken immediately to stop the condition from spreading and becoming worse. Shelter must be found and re-warming carried out. The affected tissue is damaged, and rubbing it must be avoided at all costs, as this only makes the situation worse. Rapid warming in water at a temperature of 42–43°C proves to be the best treatment. In a survival situation, you may have to make do with wrapping the affected area in damp clothes using tepid water, or body-warmed underclothing donated by the stronger members of the group.

BROKEN BONES

If conscious, a casualty with broken bones will complain of pain and will usually be unable to move the injured part properly. A broken limb may look misshapen, and swelling and bruising may be present caused by internal bleeding flooding the injury. The casualty may also complain of extreme tenderness over the break. Even if you only vaguely suspect a break, treat it as one: better safe than sorry.

> **The following action should be taken:**
>
> - Immobilize the break, which will stop the situation from becoming worse. This prevents the broken bones from rubbing together. Where possible, use a splint, otherwise immobilize the affected limb against the casualty's body.
> - Pad the limb with anything that is handy.
> - Bind the splint and broken area firmly, but not too tightly. Broken limbs swell and tight bindings restrict free blood flow. Pins and needles and numbness of the limb are signs of too tight a binding.

If you suspect a broken back, move the casualty as little as possible, making sure that he is always well-supported. Remember, nothing is impossible as long as the will to survive is present.

LONG-TERM MEDICAL PROBLEMS

After the initial first aid, medical problems will inevitably arise during the fight for survival; obviously, these will become greater with the passage of time. Personal and communal hygiene should be attended to from day one, as it is in this area that most long-term problems will arise. Most diseases, especially in the tropics, are water-borne. Always make sure that water is purified using one of the methods explained in the section on water. In warm, tropical climates, ailments caused by the sun will be the first problems to emerge, especially when the group is working to develop a comfortable camp. Once again, prevention is better than cure, and prevention starts with recognizing the symptoms of the more common ailments.

First Aid

SUNBURN

This is the reddening and eventual blistering of the skin due to ultra-violet rays. Symptoms include:

- ▲ **Pain from burning.**
- ▲ **Temporarily upset stomach.**
- ▲ **Headache.**
- ▲ **Fever.**
- ▲ **Occasional vomiting.**
- ▲ **The body's natural ability to regulate heat may be reduced because the affected areas are unable to sweat.**

There is no quick cure available; prevention is definitely better. Skin needs to develop a protective tan. In regions where the sun is very strong, exposure to it must be no longer than five minutes on the first day, gradually allowing more exposure as the days pass.

PRICKLY HEAT

Prickly heat is very common, especially in the tropics. The prickly sensation is very annoying, and plays havoc with sleep patterns. It is caused by blocking of the sweat glands, thus impairing the ability to cool the body by sweating and resulting in a more serious heat disorder. The sufferer must be kept in the shade, constantly removed from any heat stress and regularly washed with purified clean water.

HEAT EXHAUSTION

There are four separate conditions – all of which are serious – and left alone the sufferer will possibly die. These are:

Anhidrotic heat exhaustion (anhidrotic means 'without perspiration'). Symptoms include:

- The inability to sweat.
- Severe prickly heat.
- Loss of energy.
- Lack of initiative and interest.

This type of disorder is the most difficult to treat, as the sufferer does not possess the capacity to cool the body by sweating. This will cause severe dehydration, a potentially fatal condition. Make every effort to keep him cool, administering plenty of fluids.

> **Salt-deficient heat exhaustion.** This commonly occurs after two to three days of heavy sweating without sufficient salt replacement. Symptoms include:
>
> – Heavy sweating.
> – Nausea and vomiting (not always present).
> – Muscle cramps (which may involve the large muscle groups, and morphine may have to be used to relieve the severe pain).
> – Pallor.
> – Collapse.

The sufferer is in a potentially lethal situation. Rest and plenty of liquids plus salt tablets must be administered and, where possible, immediate evacuation to medical aid should be arranged. Do not give salt in water, as vomiting at this stage will be lethal.

> **Water-deficient heat exhaustion.** This usually follows periods of heavy sweating with restricted water intake. Symptoms include:
>
> – Complaints of vague discomfort.
> – No appetite.
> – Dizziness.
> – Impatience.
> – Weariness and sleepiness.
> – Tingling sensation.
> – Shortage of breath.
> – Blue tinge to the skin.
> – Difficulty in walking.

Eventually, the victim will be unable to stand or control his muscles, and hysteria and/or delirium follow. Reassurance, rest, shade and an ample supply of water promote a rapid recovery.

First Aid

> **Heat hyperprexia and heatstroke.** Those affected will be struck down rapidly and die; therefore these are potentially the most dangerous of the heat disorders.
>
> – Heat hyperprexia is a high fever defined by a body temperature of 41°C (106°F) or more. Heat-stroke is the failure of the body's heat-regulating mechanism. With heat hyperprexia, the body's heat regulating becomes impaired, resulting in a rapid progression to heat-stroke. The body temperature steadily rises in the absence of sweating, and death ensues at a temperature of approximately 43°C (109°F).

HEATSTROKE

Symptoms: the onset is sudden, with the victim showing no signs of distress even a few hours previously. The disturbances are profound:

- **Delirium**
- **Convulsions**
- **Partial or complete loss of consciousness**
- **Snoring breathing**
- **Hot, dry, flushed skin.**

The only cure is the immediate cooling of the body to check the rise in temperature. A delay of as little as two hours in this process can mean the difference between life and death.

First Aid

> **Treatment:**
>
> - Remove the victim from direct sunlight.
> - Strip him of his clothing.
> - Wrap him in a wet sheet or towel (the water should be only a couple of degrees cooler than the patient's body temperature).
> - Fan him to promote cooling by evaporation.
> - You must not apply iced water, as this fools the body into thinking it is cold. It will divert blood away from the skin and back down to the body core, making the victim's temperature sky-rocket.
> - Start the treatment as soon as you suspect heatstroke.

There is a tendency for a victim of heatstroke to crawl into a shaded area, where he may escape notice during the critical period; always be on the look out for this.

I have dealt here with the majority of heat disorders – most of which can be overcome if you are aware of them from the start. Water plays a big part in the prevention and treatment of them all.

LOCAL MEDICAL HAZARDS

In the jungle, regular medical hazards include:

▲ **Poisoning by eating or contact with vegetation.**
▲ **Malaria, dysentery, sand-fly fever and typhus.**
▲ **All animal life.**
▲ **Sun and heat.**

Prevention is better than cure. This is especially true of the jungle diseases with which you could come in contact. I have never heard of anyone dying from a disease against which he was inoculated, or for which he had had the appropriate medication before entering an infested zone. Prior to any proposed trip, check not only which areas you will be visiting, but also the areas over which you will be flying.

MALARIA AND SAND-FLY FEVER

These very similar diseases are caused by bites from an infected mosquito or sand-fly respectively. The sufferer begins by feeling chilly, usually followed by very violent shivering; the next stage is hot and cold fevers alternating throughout the illness. Rest and copious quantities of water to drink with six to eight mepacrine tablets per day should help until the patient's temperature drops. Even after this, there may be regular life-long relapses. Avoidance is by far the best bet. In both cases, the following precautions will help:

Where possible, keep away from potential infected areas. In the case of mosquitoes, these will be swampy areas. The sand-fly favours areas by rivers, in forest clearings and by the seashore. A smoky fire tends to keep them at bay, but even with the smokiest fire the insects still manage to get through. Wearing long-sleeved coats and trousers helps.

Whenever possible, construct mosquito nets and regularly spray the inside of them with an anti-insect spray. If in more temperate zones you are troubled by midges, the following concoctions will help:

- **Pine bark (Pinus) crushed into a pulp makes a good repellent.**
- **Elderberry (Sambucus nigra). Bruise some leaves and wear a sprig of them around your person; note that the green parts of this plant are poisonous.**
- **Fleabanes (Conyza). Picked and set to smoulder, these can delouse the most inaccessible areas of your shelter, but once again beware, as these are all poisonous to humans.**
- **Fly Agaric (Amanita muscaria). An infusion of 2.2lb (1kg) to 3.5 pints (2 litres) painted around the area of your camp will further help to keep at bay any insect life. Be careful, however, as this is a very potent poison and must not be eaten under any circumstances.**

DYSENTERY

This is caused by eating or drinking polluted food or water. The symptoms are severe swelling of the bowels, resulting in stomach pains and continuous diarrhoea; the faeces will be green and bloody. If you are lucky, you can treat it with sulphaguandadine. Other than this the only aid is to give the patient plenty of well-boiled water and a diet of soft food and liquids, such as boiled milk, boiled rice, coconut milk or boiled bread.

DIARRHOEA

This condition is very common in survival situations because of the type of food you will be forced to eat. Diarrhoea is not to be taken lightly, as it is a source of infection to all who are in the location, and it causes severe dehydration. Personal hygiene will keep it at bay. Treat it by resting, and drink unlimited amounts of fluid (boiled, of course). If you have any available to you, use kaolin powder; a natural alternative is peeled and grated apple, but wait until the apple turns brown (pectin) before eating it.

CONSTIPATION

This is not to be made fun of, as it can lead to very serious problems. As soon as the stools begin to be difficult to pass, drink plenty of liquid and supplement the diet with plenty of fruit and roughage. In cases of extreme – and I do mean extreme – constipation, give an enema by passing a pint of soapy solution up into the rectum, using a well-greased rubber tube. I cannot stress too much the importance of caution and the proper sterilization of equipment when this has to be undertaken.

HYGIENE

Personal and communal hygiene is absolutely vital. No one wants to live with a dirty person – except the least welcome friends such as lice and mites. Ticks are also a considerable menace and they may even swarm on to a person when disturbed. All of the above will have less effect if the body and clothing are washed regularly. The more persistent of these parasites may be dislodged by smoking: that is, hanging your clothes, or standing nude, in the path of a very smoky fire.

From time to time you may find leeches about your person; it is no use pulling them off, as all this does is detach the body from the jaws, which are then left in the skin to cause an infection. When troubled by leeches, use a smouldering stick or cigarette; they will let go in pain.

We have already mentioned the 'Buddy Buddy' system in colder regions; this system has its uses in warmer climates too. Each person should look after his mate and watch for any deterioration in his attitude and physical aptitude. They should help each other to wash properly and make sure that ablutions are performed regularly. Where a static camp has been set up, a communal latrine should be dug, along with a rubbish trench.

First Aid

POISONOUS BITES AND STINGS

Wild animals are going to present a further hazard, but you will usually hear or see them – in which case either you will keep away from them or they from you. The same applies to snakes; they, too, will leave you alone, as long as you do not disturb them. Unfortunately, they are less easy to see and you may accidentally disturb one. In the event of one of your group being bitten, the following action should be taken:

- **Reduce the spread of venom by restricting the blood flow on either side of the bite.**
- **Keep the bitten area lower than the heart.**
- **Wash the wound with soapy water.**
- **Make every effort to evacuate the casualty to a hospital as soon as possible (if you can, kill the snake and take it with you to the hospital, as it will help doctors to administer the correct anti-venom serum).**
- **Stop the victim from making any form of movement, as this will quicken the blood flow and force the venom around the body more quickly.**
- **The pain must be treated, and reassurance given to the victim.**
- **The cobra can spit venom into the eyes; if this happens, wash the eyes with plenty of good clean water.**

The same principles apply to any dangerously venomous bite or sting.

THE FINAL WORD

▲ The Final Word: Death

Regrettably, some accidents do result in death. Do not be too ready to diagnose death, but if it is suspected, do carry on with resuscitation for as long as possible. A dead person has no pulse, no breath and no response to tissue damage. After a while the body will chill to ambient temperature, and later decomposition will set in. Be wary of diagnosing death if there is head trauma.

If death is finally accepted, move everyone away from the body and cover it. As soon as possible, sit down and write down as much information as possible about how the person died; an inquiry will be held sooner or later, and your notes will be of great use. Other members of the group may be upset at the death, and you should busy yourself by attending to them. Death is an inevitable part of living, and overreaction to it only makes the situation worse.

Although I have already mentioned cannibalism, I think it is worth reiterating the dilemma here. In the fight for life, many a survivor has lived by eating a dead person. This action is shunned by the majority of civilized people but, faced with the prospect of death by starvation, I believe that few of us would not eventually eat another who, after all, was already dead and no longer in need of a body. If you did not eat a fallen comrade and subsequently died, then this would be a waste of two lives rather than one.

I for one would expect to be eaten if my body was lying there going bad while my former companions were starving.

APPENDIX

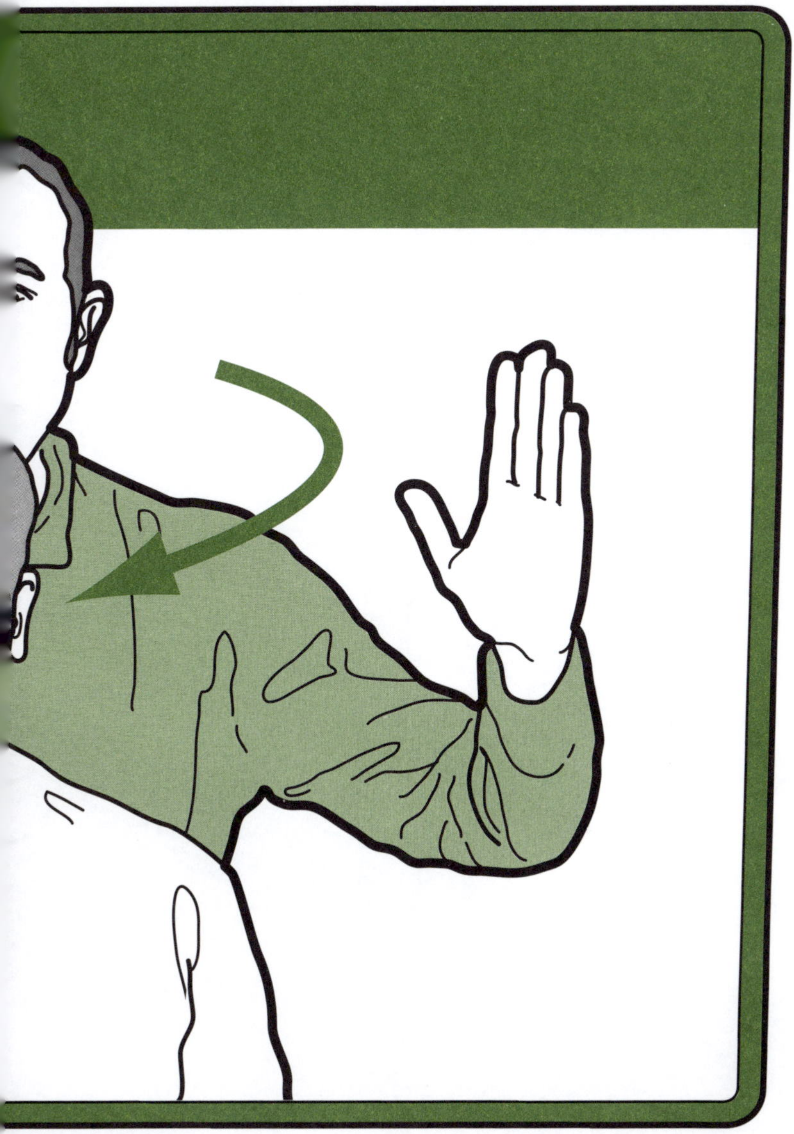

Distress Signals

Need medical assistance

Affirmative (Yes)

Distress Signals

Our receiver is operating

Use drop message

Distress Signals

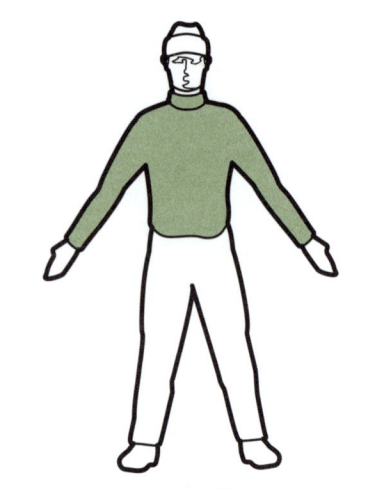

Negative (No)

Do not attempt to land here

Distress Signals

All OK, do not wait

Land here

Distress Signals

Can proceed shortly, wait if practicable

Need mechanical help or parts

Distress Signals

Plane abandoned

Distress Signals

Message	Pyrotechnic	Audible	Visual
I want help	1 red or succession of reds (A)	Mountain distress signal (C) or SOS whistle (E)	Pyro signal Mountain distress signal SOS (lightly) (C)
Message understood (B)	1 white or succession of whites used by party on the hill (A)	Mountain distress (D)	Mountain distress (D)
Position of base camp	1 white or yellow or a succession of whites or yellows	No audible signal to be used	Steady white or yellow light(s) (car head spot or search lights pointed upwards if possible)
Recall to base camp	A succession of greens	A succession of thunder-flashes, notes on horn, bell, whistle etc	A succession of white or yellow light(s) swtiched on and off (or a long-burning flare)

A) Thunder-flashes should be used to attract attention before signalling.

B) Message understood. It is not always advisable to send a reply or to make the 'Message understood' code. It may cause those in distress to stop signalling before their position is accurately fixed.

C) Mountain distress signal. Six long calls, flashes, whistles, etc, in quick succession, repeated at one-minute intervals.

D) Mountain distress reply. Three long calls, flashes, whistles, etc, in quick succession, repeated at one-minute intervals.

E) SOS. Three short, three long and three short calls, flashes, whistles etc (...---...)

Natural North Indicators

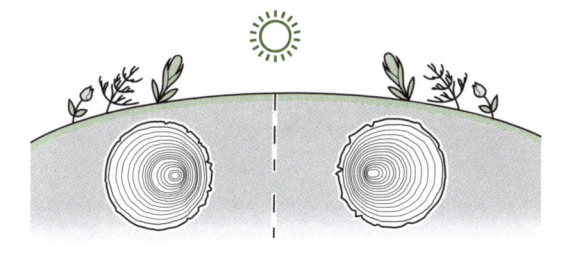

Plants grow towards the sun. When cut, tree rings are closers together on the sunnier side. Bark has more cracks on the sunnier side.

Prevailing winds cause plant life to lean away from them. Forests have shorter tree growth on the windward side.

Sand dunes and sand banks behind plant life give a clue of the prevailing winds.

Stars in the Northern Hemisphere

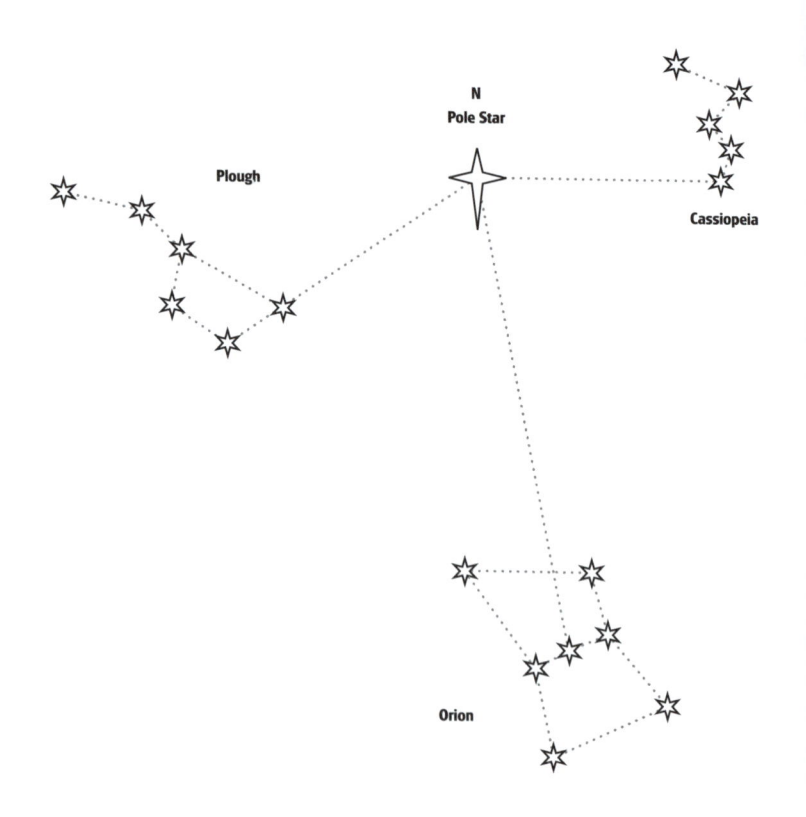

N
Pole Star

Plough

Cassiopeia

Orion

Stars in the Southern Hemisphere

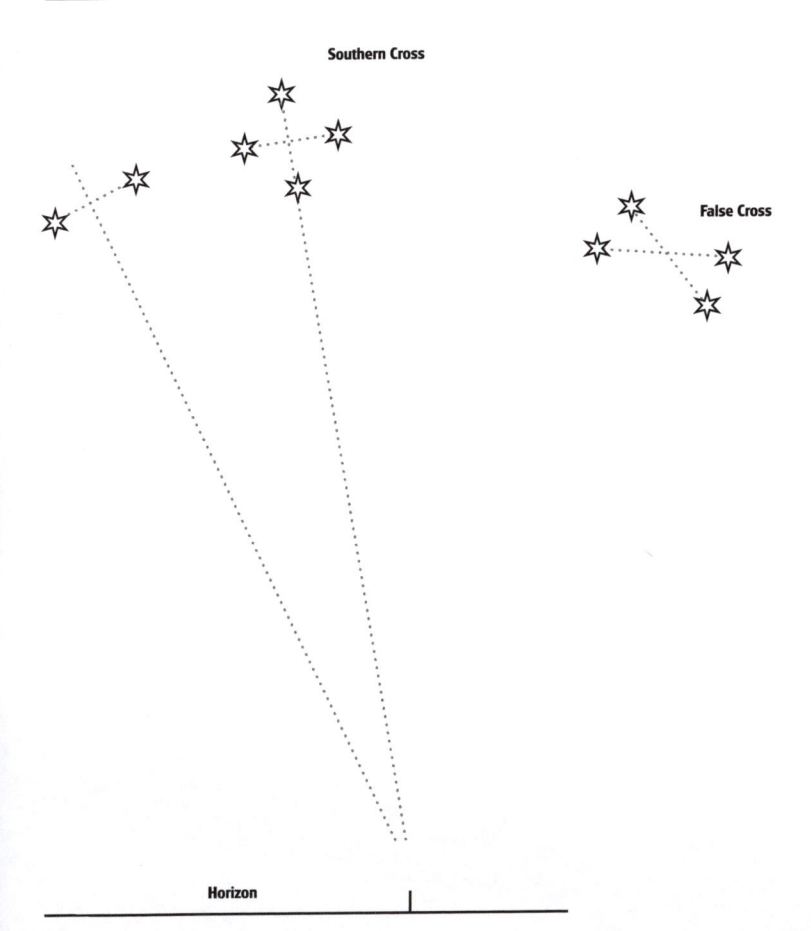

Southern Cross

False Cross

Horizon

Index

abseiling 103–5
accident procedure 156
air travel 149–50
assertive communication 17–19
attracting attention 107-09
avalanches 151–2
awareness, development of 20, 46–7

back-break throw 60
batteries 118
birds
    cooking 129
    dressing 139
    traps for 134–35
bites 172
biting 52
bleeding 160
boat capsizing 34–7
bodily needs
    water 100–06
bombs 71–2
bones, broken 165
bow-drill 121
building a shelter 28–9

candles 118
cannibalism 141, 174–5
car-jacking 146-5
car theft 147
cars *see also* vehicles
    car-jacking 146–7
    evasive driving 147
    flat tyre scams 147–8
    theft 147
cigarette lighters 117, 124
climates
    cold 30-2, 162–4
    cold and wet 31–2
    heat loss 30
    hot 33, 166–9
    salt loss 33
    wind chill 32
climbing 103–5
clothing
    in cold climates 31–2
cold climate survival 30-2, 162–4
communication, non verbal 16–17
compasses 86, 88–91
constipation 171
cooking
    equipment 130–31
    methods 128–9
crustacean cooking 128
currents 37–8
cyber threats 78–84

death 174–5
defence stance 51
desert shelters 28
diarrhoea 171
direction finding 86, 93-5, 185–87
disaster recovery, cyber 84
distress signals 108–9, 178–84
dysentery 170

ear-slap 61
earthworms, eating 141
electromagnetic pulse 79–81
evasive
    driving 147
    movement 153–4
exposure 161–2
external chest compression 158–9

Index

fighting back 49–50
filtering water 116
finger-jab 54
fire
    fire extinguishers 43
    fuel 124
    indoor 44
    kindling 122
    lighting 117–22, 124
    outdoor 45
    pit fires 125
    poacher's boiling fire 126
    poacher's griddle fire 127
    preparing 122
    pyramid fires 126
    rescue 96
    siting 123
    smoke alarms 43
    vehicle 44
fire extinguishers 43
firelighters 120
first aid
    accident procedure 156
    bites 172
    bleeding 160
    broken bones 165
    cold-weather protocol 162–3
    constipation 171
    diarrhoea 171
    dysentery 170
    exposure 161–2
    external chest compression 158–9
    frostbite 163–4
    heat exhaustion 166–8
    heatstroke 168–9
    kits 155–6
    malaria 170
    mouth to mouth resuscitation 156–8
    prickly heat 166
    sand-fly fever 170
    shock 160–1
    stings 172
    sunburn 166
    unconsciousness 159–60
fish
    cooking 128–9
    dressing 138
    traps for 135–6
fists 52
firewalls 82
flat tyre scams 147–8
flood survival 40
food preparation
    animals 139–40
    birds 139
    fish 138
    rats 140
frostbite 163–4
fruit cooking 129
fuel 124

game traps 136–7
Great Plantain 142
grid letters 88
gun attacks 62–3

hair 58
hands for self-defence 53
Hawthorns 143
head butt 52
heat exhaustion 166–8
heat loss 30–3
heatstroke 168
herb cooking 129
hijacking 64–7
hitchhiking 144–5
hot climate survival 33, 166–9
hygiene, importance of 171

inflatable boats 36–7
information protection 80–84

jungle shelters 25

kicking 54–5
kidnapping
    avoidance 70
    escaping 69–70
    surviving 68–9
    tying up 67–8

vehicle escape 70
kindling 122
kneeing 54
knife attacks 56, 59, 61

lens 118
letter bombs 72
lightning 24–5

malaria 170
mammals
    cooking 129
    dressing 139–40
    traps for 136–7
map reading 85, 86–8, 90–2
matches 117, 124
moorland shelters 25–6
mouth to mouth resuscitation 156–8

navigation
    compasses 86, 88–91
    direction finding 86, 93–5, 185–87
    map reading 85, 86–8, 90–2
    ocean 92
    self-rescue 101
new threats 78–84
non verbal communication 16–17

ocean navigation 92

packs 98
password attack 83
parcel bombs 72
phishing 83
pit fires 125
plants
    edible 142–3
    medicinal 12, 142–3
poacher's boiling fire 126
poacher's griddle fire 127
poisonous animals, eating 141
preparation 10–13
prickly heat 166
psychology of self-defence 13–15
pump-drill 121–2

purifying water 113
pyramid fires 126

rats, dressing 140
rear hair hold 58
reptiles
    cooking 129
    dressing 139–40
rescue
    attempts 66
    fires 96–7
    resting 105–6
    river crossing 38–40
root cooking 129
Rosebay Willow Herb 142
Run, Hide, Tell 74–76

salt loss 33
sand-fly fever 170
sea travel 150–1
self-defence
    back-break throw 60
    biting 52
    defence stance 51
    ear-slap 61
    edge of the hand 53
    fighting back 49–50
    finger-jab 54
    fists 52
    gun attacks 62–3
    head butt 52
    heel of the hand 53
    kicking 54–5
    knees 54
    knife attacks 56, 59, 61
    psychology of 14–15
    rear hair hold 58
    strangleholds 57, 59
self-rescue
    briefing 99–102
    climbing 119–20
    group 115–117
    leaving trails 99
    navigation 101
    packs 98

Index

    resting 105–6
    route planning 97–8
    time estimation 98
    walking 106
shelters
    building 28–9
    choosing a site 22–3
    desert 28
    jungle 25
    lightning 24–5
    moorland 25–6
    snow 26–7
    tree 24–5
    types of 21–2
    woodland 24
shipwrecks 150–1
shock 160–1
signalling 107–9, 178–83
smoke alarms 43
snails, eating 141
snow shelters 26–7
solar stills 112–3
Stinging Nettles 142
stings 172
strangleholds 57, 59
street survival
    awareness 46–7
    being followed 47
    minimizing risk 47–8
sunburn 166
sunken vehicle survival 41–2
survival kits 10–13
swamp survival 41
swimming 38

taxis 148
terrorism
    bombs 71–2
    communicating with 65–6
    hijacking 64–7
    kidnapping 68–70
    surviving 73–77
tides 37–8
trails 99
trains 148

trapping
    bird traps 134–5
    rules of 132–4
tree shelters 24–5

unconsciousness 159–60
vehicles *see also* cars
    attack from 76–77
    fire 44
    kidnapping in 68
    sunken 41–2
volcanoes 152

walking 106
water
    filtering 116
    locating 114–16
    purification 113
    rationing 111
    shortages 110–11
    solar stills 112–3
water survival
    capsizing boats 34–7
    currents 37–8
    floods 40
    inflatable boats 36–7
    navigation 92
    river crossing 38–40
    sunken vehicles 41–2
    swamps 41
    swimming 38
    tides 37–8
water-fowl traps 135
wind chill 32
woodland shelters 24